USING TECHNOLOGY
with CLASSROOM INSTRUCTION *that* Works

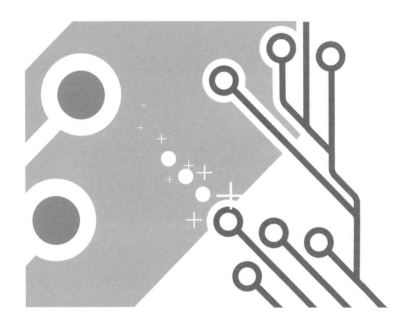

Howard Pitler

Elizabeth R. Hubbell

Matt Kuhn

Kim Malenoski

Alexandria, Virginia USA

Mid-continent Research for
Education and Learning
Denver, Colorado USA

1703 N. Beauregard St. • Alexandria, VA 22311-1714 USA
Phone: 800-933-2723 or 703-578-9600 • Fax: 703-575-5400
Web site: www.ascd.org E-mail: member@ascd.org
Author guidelines: www.ascd.org/write

Mid-continent Research for Education and Learning

4601 DTC Boulevard, Suite 500 • Denver, Colorado 80237 USA
Telephone: 303-337-0990 • Fax: 303-337-3005
Web site: www.mcrel.org E-mail: info@mcrel.org

Gene R. Carter, *Executive Director;* Nancy Modrak, *Director of Publishing;* Julie Houtz, *Director of Book Editing & Production;* Katie Martin, *Project Manager;* Catherine Guyer, *Senior Graphic Designer;* Valerie Younkin, *Desktop Publishing Specialist;* Dina Murray Seamon, *Production Specialist/Team Lead*

All Web links in this book are correct as of the publication date below but may have become inactive or otherwise modified since that time. If you notice a deactivated or changed link, please e-mail books@ascd.org with the words "Link Update" in the subject line. In your message, please specify the Web link, the book title, and the page number on which the link appears.

PAPERBACK ISBN: 978-1-4166-0570-6   ASCD product #107025   s7/07

Also available as an e-book through ebrary, netLibrary, and many online booksellers (see Books in Print for the ISBNs).

Quantity discounts for the paperback edition only: 10–49 copies, 10%; 50+ copies, 15%; for 1,000 or more copies, call 800-933-2723, ext. 5634, or 703-575-5634. For desk copies, e-mail member@ascd.org.

Library of Congress Cataloging-in-Publication Data

Using technology with classroom instruction that works / Howard Pitler
. . . [et al.].
     p. cm.
  Includes bibliographical references and index.
  ISBN 978-1-4166-0570-6 (pbk. : alk. paper)   1. Educational technology
2. Effective teaching.   I. Pitler, Howard, 1952–

  LB1028.3.U849 2007
  371.33—dc22

                                        2007009085

18 17 16 15 14 13 12 11   5 6 7 8 9 10 11 12

USING TECHN○LOGY
with CLASSROOM INSTRUCTION
that Works

•ׁ+ LIST OF FIGURES

•⁺ FOREWORD

by Robert J. Marzano

U sing *Technology with Classroom Instruction That Works* is a book that is long overdue.

What's special about this book is that its authors are fluent in both the research behind the nine categories of instructional strategies presented in the book *Classroom Instruction That Works* and the ways in which technology can support and integrate these strategies. They know how to teach the strategies and why teachers need to have practical and immediately applicable solutions for their classrooms. They understand adult learning theory and the finesse necessary to teach to learners who have varying comfort levels with technology.

In addition, the authors are true educational technology leaders. Dr. Howard Pitler, an Apple Distinguished Educator and National Distinguished Principal, brings years of experience as an educator and principal of a technology magnet school. His team consists of former classroom teachers, administrators, and educational technology experts who have a very clear understanding of the changes that must take place in classrooms if we hope to meet the needs of our 21st century learners. Elizabeth R. Hubbell, a former Montessori educator, brings her expertise in discovery and experiential learning and her enthusiasm for integrating technology into the elementary classroom. Matt Kuhn, a former secondary science teacher, administrator, and national laboratory technology-outreach coordinator, conveys his understanding of and passion for using technology to teach teenagers. Kim Malenoski's experience with education at the school, district, state, and national levels have instilled in her a great commitment to giving practical guidance that makes a busy teacher's life easier. Finally, all the authors understand that a focus on technology is not "about" the technology itself, but about changing teacher practice, motivating our students, and creating learning experiences that will be applicable to their world and future workplaces.

Through practical guidance and anecdotes that put the reader right in the classroom, the authors show technology's power to reach and motivate various learners. They consistently make the points of *why* and *how* teachers should use modern technological tools to transform and energize their practice. They also make expert use of "nonlinguistic representation" in the variety of graphics, screenshots, and illustrations included throughout the book.

Perhaps this book's most powerful contribution to the field is the fact that it provides such a wide variety of resources and then *shows to which strategies those resources best apply*. For example, if your class is studying constellations, it's wonderful that you and your students can access a free, online planetarium, but what exactly is it that you want your students to *do* with this extraordinary resource? And how will the use of this resource engage your students in learning activities that have been shown to improve achievement? This book—through its structure of planning questions, categories of instructional strategies, and categories of technology—shows teachers how to think about using technology to help their students practice concepts, engage in higher-order thinking, and problem solve. In other words, it helps teachers help their students hone skills and knowledge that will serve them for the rest of their lives. That is the ultimate goal of education.

ACKNOWLEDGMENTS

This book would not have been possible without the assistance, advice, and enthusiasm of fellow educators. We would like to thank our colleagues at Mid-continent Research for Education and Learning (McREL), particularly Vicki Urquhart, for her careful editing; Linda Brannan, for her review of the manuscript and work to obtain copyright permissions; Lisa Maxfield, for keeping us organized; Brian Lancaster, for our group photo; Robert J. Marzano, for reviewing the manuscript and writing the Foreword; and Lou Cicchinelli and David Frost, for their ongoing support. We are also grateful to Rae Niles, for her writing contribution and detailed quality assurance review of the manuscript; and to Joel Solomon, for his careful insight about the manuscript during its final writing phases. A few of the examples in this book are based on activities and stories from two esteemed educators, Alan November and David Warlick, to whom we express our gratitude. We express our thanks to our editor at ASCD, Katie Martin. Finally, we would like to thank the folks at Global WRITeS, eInstruction, and Inspiration, who took extra time to help us provide best-practice examples of using technology to make a difference in student learning.

INTRODUCTION

S ince its publication in 2001, *Classroom Instruction That Works: Research-Based Strategies for Increasing Student Achievement* has sold nearly a million copies and has become standard reading material for book studies in classrooms, schools, and districts across the United States. Heeding educational leaders' call for students to "learn how to learn" in order to better prepare for the 21st century, teachers are now using a common vocabulary to pinpoint the strategies of learning that they use and teach to their students.

At Mid-continent Research for Education and Learning (McREL), our workshop based on *Classroom Instruction That Works* continues to be our most popular offering, often with standing room only. Within the educational technology department, our most requested workshop is invariably "Using Technology with Classroom Instruction That Works." Most teachers are eager to embrace new technologies, as they have seen their students' excitement and motivation increase when they do so. With technology standards becoming an integral part of students' education, teachers are more enthusiastic than ever to learn new technologies and methods. What we often hear, however, are questions and comments suggesting that teachers are uncertain about how to effectively incorporate technology into the curriculum:

• "I think the interactive games and Web sites that I find are very engaging for my students, but I'm at a loss as to how and when to use these during my teaching."

• "What skills are my students actually learning when they use science probes?"

• "Do 'drill and practice' games have any place in the classroom, or are they a waste of time for my students?"

• "I see that multimedia technology engages many different types of learners, but I'm unclear as to how to best use it to improve student achievement."

• "I know technology is important, but I just don't have the time to learn all of these new programs."

Teachers who have brought technology into their classrooms are aware that it provides an opportunity to differentiate instruction and change their classrooms into dynamic learning environments. Often, they also know that there are specific strategies that will help their students become lifelong learners. If you are one of those teachers, this book will show you the power of combining these approaches. If you are a teacher who hasn't yet begun to use technology in your classroom, don't wait any longer. Use this book to increase your knowledge and understanding of effective classroom strategies and the supporting and enhancing role that technology can play.

Throughout this book, we refer to the research and the categories of strategies described in the original *Classroom Instruction That Works*. For a detailed discussion of both, we urge you to look there.

Why Technology?

As you become more familiar with the nine categories of strategies and the profound impact that using these strategies can have on student achievement, you might ask yourself, "Why technology?" If the benefits come from using the strategies, what difference does it make which tools and resources a teacher employs in the effort?

Research indicates that technology's use in the classroom can have an additional positive influence on student learning when the learning goals are clearly articulated prior to the technology's use (Ringstaff & Kelley, 2002; Schacter, 1999). Applied effectively, technology implementation not only increases student learning, understanding, and achievement but also augments motivation to learn, encourages collaborative learning, and supports the development of critical thinking and problem-solving skills (Schacter & Fagnano, 1999).

Russell and Sorge (1999) also point to how technology can give students "more control over their own learning," facilitating the analytical and critical thinking and the collaboration championed in the constructivist approach to education (pp. 1–2). Their conclusion—that integrating technology into instruction tends to move classrooms from teacher-dominated environments to ones that are more student-centered—is supported repeatedly in the literature. Although student achievement outcomes in these learning environments are difficult to measure because many existing assessments do not adequately capture higher-order thinking skills, in such constructivist classrooms, students tend to work cooperatively, have more opportunities to make choices, and play a more active role in their learning (Mize & Gibbons, 2000; Page, 2002; Waxman, Connell, & Gray, 2002). Furthermore, technology allows teachers to differentiate instruction more efficiently by providing a wider variety of avenues for learning that reach students of divergent readiness levels, interests, and learning styles.

Some of the differences in how learning occurs in technology-rich classrooms as contrasted with traditional classrooms may account for consistent findings that technology can be especially effective with at-risk and special needs students. A research synthesis conducted by McREL suggests that computer-assisted instruction (known as CAI) contributes to the learning of at-risk students for a number of reasons: It is nonjudgmental and motivational; facilitates frequent and immediate feedback; allows teachers to individualize learning through designs to meet students' needs; allows for more student autonomy; and provides a multisensory learning environment incorporating images, sounds, and symbols (Barley et al., 2002, p. 97).

As we know, Benjamin Bloom created a taxonomy of learning activities that range from simple, factual recall of material to the application and evaluation of concepts. The taxonomy has since been revised to reflect cognitive processes (Anderson & Krathwohl, 2001; Cochran, Conklin, & Modin, 2007) (see Figure 1). Technology can certainly be used to provide immediate feedback for drill and practice, but it can also be used as a tool for the analysis, synthesis, and evaluation of information. Today, students use complex multimedia products and advanced networking technologies to learn interactively and work collaboratively on projects; to gather, organize, and analyze information; to solve problems; and to communicate information (Ringstaff & Kelley, 2002).

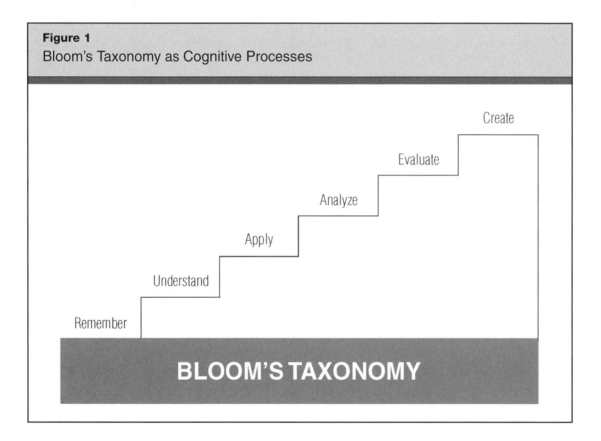

Figure 1
Bloom's Taxonomy as Cognitive Processes

Create

Evaluate

Analyze

Apply

Understand

Remember

BLOOM'S TAXONOMY

Robert J. Marzano and John S. Kendall (2007) offer another perspective in their New Taxonomy of Educational Objectives, which incorporates a wide range of factors involved with students' thinking and learning. This taxonomy is an intersecting matrix of three systems of thought and three knowledge domains. When a student starts a new task, the *self system* decides whether to continue the current behavior or engage in the new activity; the *metacognitive system* sets goals and monitors progress, clarity, and accuracy; the *cognitive system* processes information; and the *knowledge domains* (information, mental procedures, and psychomotor procedures) provide the content. Technology can potentially play a role within any of the systems, but seems to especially support the cognitive system by helping students to comprehend, apply, and recall concepts.

Dr. Rae Niles, director of curriculum and technology for Sedgwick Public Schools (USD 439) in Kansas, tells this story to illustrate the effect that technology can have on student learning:

> Educators from more than 45 different school districts came to visit our high school during the first year of our one-to-one laptop computer initiative. Most came thinking they were going to see the technology, and left realizing it wasn't really about the technology at all. It was about the teaching and the learning and how the technology had transformed what was occurring within the school walls.
>
> Typically, when visitors arrive at our school, we conduct a 25- to 30-minute impromptu tour of the facilities, allowing for spontaneous conversations with faculty and students. Following the tour, the visitors have a chance to speak with a "panel of experts": Ten students of varying academic track records and socioeconomic backgrounds, ranging in age from 16 to 18.
>
> During one visit, the superintendent from a neighboring school district turned to one of the students and said, in a very accusatory tone, "So, how is this [the one-to-one laptop computer access] really making a difference for you?"
>
> The young man, Casey, looked the superintendent squarely in the eyes and replied, "Sir, I'm special ed, and I've been special ed all my life. But with this thing here," he said, pointing to his laptop computer, "with this, I am just as smart as the next kid."
>
> To say you could hear a pin drop was an understatement. Those in the room sat in stunned silence. The superintendent recoiled and immediately asked, "No, really. How is it making a difference for you?"
>
> Casey responded: "I don't read so well, and learning through my eyes is hard. With the laptop, what I do is write what I am going to turn in, like an essay or answers to the questions the teacher has on the assignment, and then I go up to the menu bar and pull down to 'speak it.' Then I put on my headphones, close my eyes, and listen as the computer reads back to me what I have written. If what I have written makes sense, then I know what I have written is OK to hand in. If not, then I can go back and make my corrections."
>
> Casey was a senior who had been placed in special education as a 1st grader. For almost 12 years, his learning style had been controlled by his teachers, reflecting the way that they assumed he learned best. But

technology had allowed Casey to use his strengths to learn in the way he *actually* learned best. It helped him believe he could be successful. Casey went on to graduate from high school and to complete a two-year fire science degree from a nearby community college. He now works as a firefighter/EMT and was married this past spring.

It is our intention, with this book, to show teachers effective ways to use the dynamic technology tools available to them to enrich students' learning experiences, encourage project-based instruction, and give students the skills they need to become lifelong learners and critical thinkers. Before exploring these technologies, however, a brief review of the research underlying our recommendations will be helpful.

Research from *Classroom Instruction That Works*

Researchers at McREL analyzed and synthesized the results of more than 100 research reports on instruction from the past 30 years to identify categories of instructional strategies that have the most profound effect on student achievement. The analysis revealed nine categories of instructional strategies that have a high probability of enhancing student achievement for *all students,* in *all subject areas,* and at *all grade levels.* A report describing the findings, *A Theory-Based Meta-Analysis of Research on Instruction,* was published in 1998. A PDF of the 172-page report is available at www.mcrel.org/instructionmetaanalysis.

In 2001, Robert J. Marzano, Debra Pickering, and Jane E. Pollock wrote *Classroom Instruction That Works: Research-Based Strategies for Increasing Student Achievement.* This book presents the research and theory behind the categories of instructional strategies first identified in McREL's 1998 report and also offers explicit examples, suggestions for classroom practice, and advice for instructional planning. The authors explain how researchers used a technique known as *meta-analysis* to identify the strategies. A meta-analysis combines the results from a number of studies to determine the average effect of a given technique. Combining the pools of subjects in a number of studies yields data that are much more meaningful than those generated by studies with smaller sample sizes. When conducting a meta-analysis, a researcher translates the results of a given study into a unit of measurement referred to as an *effect size*. An effect size expresses the increase or decrease in achievement of the group that received the intervention in terms of standard deviation units.

For example, an effect size of 1.0 means that the average score for students in the experimental group is 1.0 standard deviation higher than the average score of students in the control group. An effect size can be translated into a *percentile gain*. Percentile gains are related to the normal distribution or "bell curve" of student achievement score distribution.

An effect size of 1.0 calculates to a percentile gain of 34 points. So, if a control group scored at the 50th percentile, and the experimental group had an effect size of 1.0, the experimental group would score at the 84th percentile (see Figure 2).

Figure 3 lists the nine categories of instructional strategies that showed strong effects on student achievement, along with the

Figure 2
Effect Size of 1.0 Showing a Percentile Gain of 34

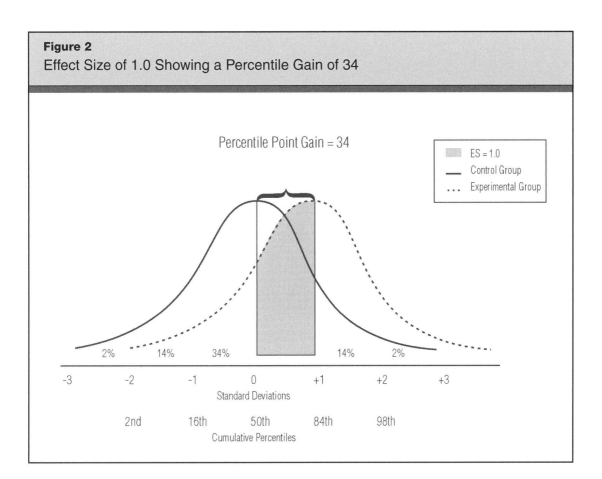

Figure 3
The Nine Categories of Instructional Strategies
That Affect Student Achievement

Strategy	Average Effect Size	Percentile Gain	Number of Studies
1. Identifying similarities and differences	1.61	45	31
2. Summarizing and note taking	1.00	34	179
3. Reinforcing effort and providing recognition	.80	29	21
4. Homework and practice	.77	28	134
5. Nonlinguistic representation	.75	27	246
6. Cooperative learning	.73	27	122
7. Setting objectives and providing feedback	.61	23	408
8. Generating and testing hypotheses	.61	23	63
9. Cues, questions, and advance organizers	.59	22	1251

corresponding average effect size, percentile gain, and number of studies included.

The effect size and percentile gains represent an average of the total effect sizes and percentile gains within each category. This means that the effect sizes in some of the studies could have been smaller or larger than the effect size shown here. In other words, although each of these categories has been shown to boost student achievement, none works equally well in all situations.

Figure 4 presents McREL's definitions of the nine categories of strategies. When teachers look over this list, they typically notice that these are strategies they already use. Indeed, seasoned teachers are masters of questioning, helping students to set goals, providing feedback, and giving students the tools they need to understand concepts. The purpose of the research is to help teachers hone their craft: Identify the strategies more precisely, use the strategies more purposefully, and ultimately, improve student learning.

Figure 4
The Instructional Strategies Defined

Category	Definition
1. Identifying similarities and differences	Enhance students' understanding of and ability to use knowledge by engaging them in mental processes that involve identifying ways items are alike and different.
2. Summarizing and note taking	Enhance students' ability to synthesize information and organize it in a way that captures the main ideas and supporting details.
3. Reinforcing effort and providing recognition	Enhance students' understanding of the relationship between effort and achievement by addressing students' attitudes and beliefs about learning. Provide students with rewards or praise for their accomplishments related to the attainment of a goal.
4. Homework and practice	Extend the learning opportunities for students to practice, review, and apply knowledge. Enhance students' ability to reach the expected level of proficiency for a skill or process.
5. Nonlinguistic representation	Enhance students' ability to represent and elaborate on knowledge using mental images.
6. Cooperative learning	Provide students with opportunities to interact with each other in groups in ways that enhance their learning.
7. Setting objectives and providing feedback	Provide students a direction for learning and information about how well they are performing relative to a particular learning goal so that they can improve their performance.
8. Generating and testing hypotheses	Enhance students' understanding of and ability to use knowledge by engaging them in mental processes that involve making and testing hypotheses.
9. Cues, questions, and advance organizers	Enhance students' ability to retrieve, use, and organize what they already know about a topic.

Four Planning Questions for Instruction

As more and more teachers learn about the nine categories of effective instructional strategies, many ask if McREL offers any guidance regarding when to use a particular strategy. The answer is yes. Four questions frame the nine categories of strategies, and McREL's research shows that certain strategies are more appropriate for responding to certain questions. The following planning questions should guide teachers in aligning curriculum, instruction, and assessment:

1. What will students learn?
2. Which strategies will provide evidence of student learning?
3. Which strategies will help students acquire and integrate learning?
4. Which strategies will help students practice, review, and apply learning?

Each of the categories of instructional strategies relates to at least one of these questions. We should mention that since the publication of *Classroom Instruction That Works,* McREL has split some of the original categories, such as *reinforcing effort and providing recognition,* into two distinct strategies to more accurately reflect the different purposes each serves during the planning stages of a unit. As shown in Figure 5, some strategies apply to more than one planning question; in this book we address each strategy and related technologies only once, as a chapter in the question-specific section where the strategy first appears.

Research shows that effective teaching results in impressive gains for student achievement, regardless of prior achievement (Goodwyn, 1999). As teachers well know, the majority of their teaching time and the strategies that they use fall within helping students

Figure 5

The Four Planning Questions and Corresponding Instructional Strategies

Part	Planning Questions	Instructional Strategies	Chapter
I	What will students learn?	• Setting objectives	1
II	Which strategies will provide evidence of student learning?	• Providing feedback • Providing recognition	2 3
III	Which strategies will help students acquire and integrate learning?	• Cues, questions, and advance organizers • Nonlinguistic representation • Summarizing and note taking • Cooperative learning • Reinforcing effort	4 5 6 7 8
IV	Which strategies will help students practice, review, and apply learning?	• Identifying similarities and differences • Homework and practice • Generating and testing hypotheses	9 10 11

to "acquire and integrate new knowledge." For this reason, Section III is this book's longest, comprising five chapters of strategies and technologies to help teachers during this most crucial step in planning for instruction. Figure 5 provides a comprehensive map of where we address each strategy in this book.

Pairing Technology and Effective Instructional Strategies

In the article "Building Better Instruction," McREL consultants Kathy Brabec, Kim Fisher, and Howard Pitler (2004) outline how technology could be used to complement and enhance the nine categories of teaching strategies. The authors group technology into five genres— *word processing applications, organizing and brainstorming software, multimedia, data collection tools,* and *Web resources*—and provide examples of how these various types of technology supported the nine categories of strategies. Since that article's publication, McREL has added two additional genres of technology to the list: *spreadsheet software* and *communication software.* Figure 6 lists the seven categories of technology along with definitions and examples of each.

Our experience has shown that most people prefer exploring the instructional strategies first and the technologies that support them second. For this reason, we have organized this book by the overarching planning questions, then by the categories of instructional strategies that correspond to those planning questions, and finally by the technologies that best support those strategies. To ensure that our matrix will endure over time as new technologies emerge, we have grouped the various technologies by function (see Figure 7). Please note that although there are seven identified genres of technologies, not all apply to every strategy. Furthermore, the technology examples we present throughout the book are not a comprehensive listing of all possible ways in which technology can be used in the classroom; rather, they serve as guiding examples of how teachers can use hardware and software that is readily accessible in their daily work. We understand that individual teachers' decisions about technology integration will reflect the technology available, their students' facility with that technology, the curricular goals pursued, and the time available.

Figure 6
The Seven Categories of Technology

Technology Category	Definition	Examples
Word processing applications	Software that enables the user to type and manipulate text	Microsoft Word, OpenOffice.org Writer, Google Docs, MYAccess!
Spreadsheet software	Software that enables the user to type and manipulate numbers	Microsoft Excel, OpenOffice.org Calc, InspireData, Google Spreadsheets
Organizing and brainstorming software	Software that enables the user to create idea maps, KWHL charts, and category maps	Inspiration, Kidspiration, BrainStorm, SMART Ideas, Visual Mind
Multimedia	Software that enables the user to create or access visual images, text, and sound in one product	iMovie, Microsoft Movie Maker, Adobe Photoshop, Microsoft PowerPoint, KidPix Studio, Keynote, OpenOffice.org, Impress
Data collection tools	Hardware and software that enable the user to gather data	Probeware, USB microscopes, classroom response systems
Web resources	Resources available on the Web that enable the user to gather information or apply or practice a concept	Virtual tours, information, applets, movies, pictures, simulations
Communication software	Software that enables the user to communicate via text, presentation, voice, or a combination of the three	Blogs, e-mail, VoIP, podcasts, wikis

How to Get the Most from This Book

Within each of this book's question-focused parts, each chapter follows a similar structure. We begin with a short overview of the selected strategy, followed by generalizations from the research and specific recommendations for using the strategy in the classroom. We then provide specific examples of technologies that support the strategy. All chapters include teacher- and student-created examples, many of which reflect actual lesson plans, projects, and products.

Throughout, we also give specific directions for when to use the tools, how they help students to use learning strategies, and which tools work best for each task. We have kept our directions for skill-based use of the hardware or software minimal, as we truly want this

Figure 7

Matrix of the Four Planning Questions, the Nine Categories of Instructional Strategies, and the Seven Categories of Technology

Planning Questions	Instructional Strategies	Word Processing Applications	Spreadsheet Software	Organizing and Brainstorming Software	Data Collection Tools	Multimedia	Web Resources	Communication Software
What will students learn?	Setting objectives	●		●	●		●	●
Which strategies will provide evidence of student learning?	Providing feedback	●			●		●	●
	Providing recognition				●	●	●	●
Which strategies will help students acquire and integrate learning?	Cues, questions, and advance organizers	●	●	●		●		
	Nonlinguistic representation	●	●	●	●	●	●	
	Summarizing and note taking	●		●		●	●	●
	Cooperative learning					●	●	●
	Reinforcing effort		●		●			
Which strategies will help students practice, review, and apply learning?	Identifying similarities and differences	●	●	●	●			
	Homework and practice	●	●			●	●	●
	Generating and testing hypotheses		●		●		●	

book to be a practical guide rather than a procedural manual. The directions we do provide reflect the most current iterations of these products at the time of this book's publication. For step-by-step instructions on using the various software and hardware, we recommend consulting Atomic Learning (www.atomiclearning.com) or Recipes4Success (www.myt4l.com). These subscription-based resources provide short, simple instructions, with screen shots and voiceovers, for performing a variety of tasks with many programs. For a more structured classroom environment, educators might take a short course offered at many computer retailers and most community colleges. And although we have tried to keep the software and hardware we discuss generic, at times we do mention products by name and talk about their particular features. Links to these resources can be found in the References section.

The book concludes with a focus on how to plan for technology in the classroom. We discuss the national technology standards for both teachers and students and include a lesson plan template that weds curriculum with standards and technology. Teachers, technology leaders, and administrators will find directions for implementing a technology initiative into their school or district, and teachers will find a technology integration rubric to use to see how far they've progressed on the road to technology integration.

Technology can transform teaching and learning. Collected in this book are a number of truly useful educational tools and examples, aligned to research-proven teaching strategies. Used as we have described, this technology can move you from a good teacher to a great teacher and give you the positive influence on student learning you have always hoped for.

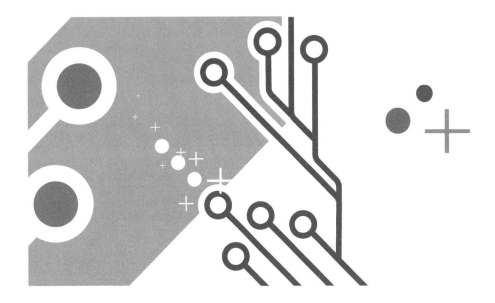

I. What Will Students Learn?

At the start of the planning process, the first question for a teacher to answer is usually the most obvious: *What knowledge and skills do I want my students to have at the end of this lesson or unit?* To answer this question, you must know the specific standards, benchmarks, and supporting knowledge that students are supposed to learn. *Setting objectives* is the instructional strategy to use during this phase of planning, and it is the focus of Chapter 1.

1

SETTING OBJECTIVES

The instructional strategy of *setting objectives* focuses on establishing a direction for learning. Setting goals or objectives is a skill that successful people have mastered to help them realize both short-term and long-term accomplishments.

McREL's research on setting objectives supports the following generalizations:

GENERALIZATIONS

1. Setting instructional goals narrows what students focus on.
2. Teachers should encourage students to personalize the learning goals the teacher has identified for them.
3. Instructional goals should not be too specific.

Based on these findings, we have four recommendations for classroom practice:

RECOMMENDATIONS

1. Set learning objectives that are specific but flexible.

2. Allow students flexibility in personalizing the learning objectives or goals.
3. Communicate the learning objectives or goals to students and parents.
4. Contract with students to attain specific learning objectives or goals.

Research shows that when students are allowed to set some of their own learning goals, their motivation is higher than when they pursue only teacher-set goals (Hom & Murphy, 1983). Technology enhances the goal-setting process by providing organizational and communication tools that make it easier to clarify the learning objectives. Technology also gives teachers access to resources that can help them identify and refine standards and objectives. In this chapter, we show how to use the following technologies to set objectives: *word processing applications, organizing and brainstorming software, data collection tools, Web resources,* and *communication software.*

○ Word Processing Applications

Many teachers already use a computer to write their lesson and unit plans and are familiar with the basics of word processing. A natural next step for teachers is to be more mindful of setting objectives when they begin to develop a unit or lesson, and to prompt their students to think about setting objectives as well. There are several ways that a word processor can help teachers and students set goals more effectively.

One method that many educators use is to have students create a KWHL chart, which prompts individual students to record what they *k*now about a topic, what they *w*ant to learn about that topic, *h*ow they plan to learn it, and what they *l*earned at the end of the unit or activity. This is a great way to activate prior knowledge and to have students personalize their learning goals—one of the research-based classroom recommendations.

The draw tools in most word processing programs make creating KWHL charts quite easy. In Microsoft Word, the draw toolbar is located on the bottom of the screen and also at View > Toolbars > Drawing. In Appleworks, the draw palette is visible when you click on the Draw button on the button bar. As Figure 1.1 illustrates, creating a

KWHL chart in a word processing program is simply a matter of drawing four vertical rectangles and then keying the appropriate letter in each box.

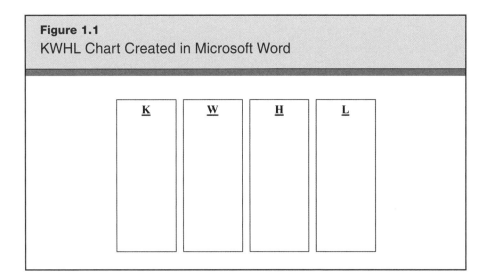

Figure 1.1
KWHL Chart Created in Microsoft Word

Why go through the effort to create an electronic chart when it would be easy enough to just draw one on a piece of paper? Look again at the third classroom recommendation for setting objectives, listed on page 18: to communicate these goals with both students and parents. If the KWHL chart is electronic, it can be e-mailed to parents in a newsletter or even posted to the school's Web site.

To transform a Microsoft Word document into a Web page, just click File > Save As, and then select Web Page (htm, html) in the pull-down menu at the bottom of the dialog box. The document is now in HTML format and ready to be posted to the Internet. Check with your school or district for the procedures to follow when you post to the school's Web site.

The fourth classroom recommendation in setting objectives is to create learning contracts—a step that helps to make goals more personal for students. For example, Ms. Cullen, a 7th grade social studies teacher whose class is learning about the basic structure of the government, uses a word processor to create a "learning goals sheet" (see Figure 1.2) to prompt her students to think about the class goals and set some specific goals of their own.

Figure 1.2
Learning Goal Contract Created in Microsoft Word

My Learning Goals

Our class learning goal for this unit:

To understand how "checks and balances" are designed to work.

Complete the following sentences to set your personal learning goals:

I know . . . there are three branches of government: executive, legislative, and judicial

but I want to know . . . why the legislative and executive branches are elected and the judicial isn't.

I want to know more about . . . what the Supreme Court does.

After creating this contract, Ms. Cullen can print copies and distribute them to her students to fill in by hand, or she can go one step further and save the contract as a *document template,* put it on the school server, and ask students to open and fill in the contract electronically during individual work time. The difference between a template and a regular document is that a template requires the user to save it as a new document, keeping the original unchanged. This spares the teacher the extra work of going in to fix the original whenever a student accidentally saves over it.

How do you create a document template? Like creating a Web page, this is a simple process. Click on File > Save As and then choose Document Template (.dot) from the pull-down menu.

◑ Organizing and Brainstorming Software

This family of software includes the well-known titles Kidspiration (for grades preK–5) and Inspiration (for intermediate and older students). These useful tools provide an easy way for students to plan and organize their thoughts in the beginning of a unit, during instruction, and after a unit.

Have you ever overheard a parent of one of your students ask their child, "What did you learn today?" and cringed when the student replied, "I don't know"? Allowing students to personalize their learning goals is one step toward ensuring that they understand what they are learning and why. It has the added motivating benefit of allowing students some control and voice in their learning. A very simple but effective way to help students personalize their learning goals is to create a template using Kidspiration, Inspiration, or similar organizing and brainstorming software.

As you present your broad learning objective, standard, or benchmark to your students, provide them with an organizing template that prompts them to think about what they would most like to learn and what they might focus on to meet the learning objective. The template shown in Figure 1.3, created by an Oregon high school teacher, is an example. With teacher and student learning goals in place, the lesson's purpose is clear from the outset, and the instruction that follows becomes more meaningful. End the class period by reviewing what was accomplished toward meeting the objectives.

Figure 1.3
Organizing Template Created in Inspiration

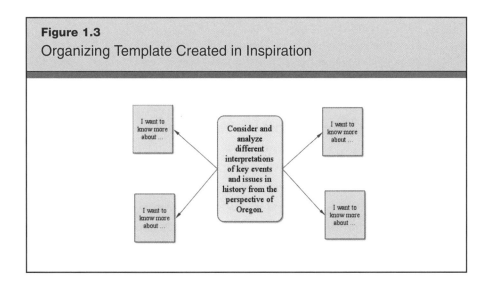

Another way to encourage students to personalize and track progress toward their learning objectives is with a KWHL template similar to the one mentioned earlier. Figure 1.4 shows an Inspiration template created by a 3rd grade teacher, Mr. Fua, who begins a unit on weather by asking his students the KWHL questions: What do you *know*? What do you *want to* know? *How* will you find out? What did you *learn*?

Mr. Fua's template illustrates the adaptability and flexibility of the software. As the students complete the chart, they create a clear visual of their current knowledge, which will help them make

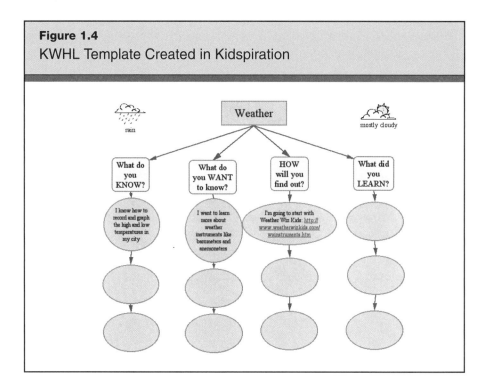

Figure 1.4
KWHL Template Created in Kidspiration

decisions about what else they would like to know. The "How will you find out?" column prompts students to plan their learning steps and to decide where and how to learn what they want to know. Students without well-developed writing skills, including younger students, those with special needs, and English language learners, may represent their current and desired knowledge by choosing from the hundreds of graphics and symbols included with both Kidspiration and Inspiration. If a desired graphic is not part of an existing symbol library, there are two ways to add it. In Kidspiration, the students can use the Symbol Maker drawing and paint tool to create practically any graphic, using a variety of lines, shapes, brushes, and colors on a "canvas." And in both Kidspiration and Inspiration, teachers can customize the symbol library by inserting, deleting, or creating a new symbol library of their choosing. This is exactly what one elementary teacher did as she was preparing her class to read the book *Knots on a Counting Rope* by Bill Martin Jr. She found graphics depicting the book cover, setting, and characters, and made a custom symbol library for her students to use. They used Kidspiration to create webs showing what they knew about the book before and after reading the story.

To install a custom graphic into a symbol library, begin by selecting the graphic that you want to install in the symbol library. Open the Symbol palette and display the library to which you want to install the graphic. Next, choose Utility > Install User Symbol. Select Standard Symbol Size or Actual Size, and then click OK. When your symbol is installed, it appears at the bottom of the Symbol palette entries and can be used just like any other symbol. (*Note:* In Kidspiration, this utility is under the Teacher menu.)

Organizing and brainstorming software often features sound components, meaning that students of all ages can also use their voices to record thoughts and ideas about their new learning. Recording a sound in Inspiration is easy. Select the symbol or topic with which you want the sound associated. Choose Tools > Sound > Record. When you are ready to record the sound or voice, choose the record button on the display. You can record up to 30 seconds of sound at one time. Be sure to save when you are finished.

Because the technology allows users to modify information, edit plans, and easily add new learning, students can work on their KWHL charts throughout a unit.

Inspiration includes two templates that are worth exploring as you work with students to personalize their learning objectives. The first is the Goal Plan template (see Figure 1.5), which comes with Inspiration version 7.5 and higher and is located in the Planning folder. Mrs. Maxfield, a middle school teacher, uses the template shown in this figure to help her students get organized for a school-wide reading challenge. Students who read five selected books and complete the requisite conference by a predetermined due date receive a $30 gift certificate to a local bookstore. As Mrs. Maxfield's students finish each book, they meet with her individually for a quick discussion and comprehension check, and to share what they enjoyed most about the book.

This is a wonderful step-by-step approach that provides a great way for students to organize their learning and set goals. It's worth noting the benefits again: Naming and dating the steps involved in meeting a goal lends concreteness to the process and increases the likelihood of accomplishing tasks.

The second Inspiration template that's useful for helping students personalize learning objectives and plan how to accomplish

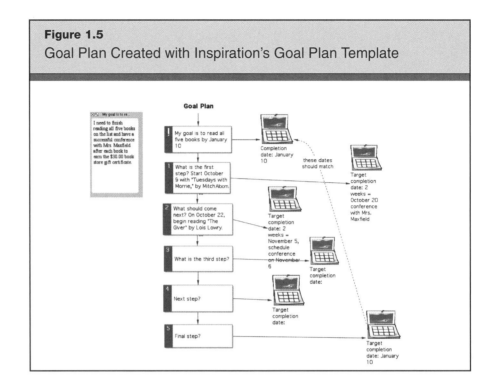

Figure 1.5
Goal Plan Created with Inspiration's Goal Plan Template

their work is called Goal Setting. It too is included with version 7.5 and higher and is located in the Planning folder. Figure 1.6 shows one of this template's possible applications. In this example, notice how student Samantha Barnes has identified her strengths and set goals for her personal learning.

One of the potential barriers to using organizing and brainstorming software is that it is not readily available on many home computers; if you were to try to e-mail a web created in this software to parents as part of efforts to further the communication of classroom learning goals, few would be able to open the file. Fortunately, there is a way around this. Both Kidspiration and Inspiration allow users to export a web as a graphic image, such as a JPEG, BMP, GIF, or PICT file.

To export an Inspiration document as an image, simply choose File > Export, then choose the Graphics File tab. This will bring up a screen asking you to choose the format in which you would like to export your Inspiration file. Your choices are GIF, JPEG, TIFF, PNG, and PICT. After you click next to the type of graphic you would like, just hit Save, and your Inspiration diagram will be converted.

Figure 1.6
Personal Learning Plan Created
with Inspiration's Goal Setting Template

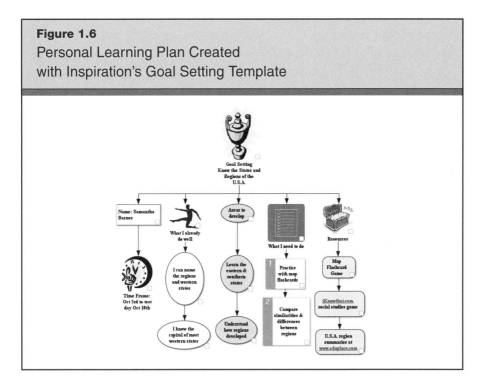

This exported graphic is a snapshot of the Inspiration file. It can be inserted into a word processing program and e-mailed to parents, providing you with another way to keep them abreast of your objectives and their child's personalized objectives and learning. Using these methods will increase the odds of hearing a more desirable response when parents ask their child, "What did you learn today?"

○ Data Collection Tools

Collecting data with online surveys allows a teacher to engage learners and gather the information needed to set more meaningful and personalized objectives. Once you learn the procedures, setting up a survey is quick and easy. Most sites allow you to archive your surveys so that you can revise and use them over again. What's more, you can collect the same survey data from multiple classes. This makes the sharing of the results with individual classes all the more powerful.

There are a few guidelines for putting together an online survey. First, consider including some engaging background information on the topic. This way, you can use the survey to activate and assess your students' prior subject knowledge. Second, be sure to include open-ended questions that will reveal any misconceptions that you might need to address. Finally, keep the survey short enough to ensure a large response and give students credit for completing it.

Here are some examples of free or inexpensive online survey Web sites:

- Survey Monkey
www.surveymonkey.com

This survey site enables anyone to create professional online surveys quickly and easily. It has a free basic service that provides most of the features a teacher would need to survey students.

- Pollcat
www.pollcat.com

The free version of Pollcat is called Pollcat Lite. It provides an easy-to-learn interface to allow you to get your survey on the Web quickly. You can view/download survey summary reports, receive automatic e-mail notifications with your survey summary reports, and review/download each of the individual survey responses.

- Web Surveyor
www.websurveyor.com/free-survey-tools.asp

Here, you'll find a link to RSVME, a free application that integrates with Microsoft Outlook and other e-mail packages to make obtaining feedback from people a snap. You can quickly and easily put together a questionnaire on any subject.

- Profiler Pro
www.profilerpro.com

This comprehensive survey tool was developed to help K–16 educators measure both the effect of integrating new technology into learning environments and the effect of comprehensive staff development programs.

What does the use of data collection tools to inform goal setting look like in the classroom? Consider the example of Mr. Solomon, a 7th grade social studies teacher whose curriculum standards include many learning objectives about World War II. Mr. Solomon wants to focus his World War II unit on the decisions of important civilian and military leaders and the major turning points in the war. One of these turning points was the Battle of Leyte Gulf, one of the last major battleship engagements in world history. This sea battle's outcome left the Japanese islands and mainland coast unprotected by any significant Japanese naval or air power.

There are many paths this lesson might take. Mr. Solomon decides to use Survey Monkey to create a pre-assessment survey that will engage his students and help him assess their prior knowledge, identify their misconceptions, and focus the class objectives based on their preferences. His survey lists five possible class objectives based on his curriculum standards and features an introduction he wrote based on research from The Battleship Page (www.battleship. org/html/Articles/History/History.htm). Mr. Solomon e-mails the survey to students to complete as a homework assignment and arranges for students who do not have Internet access at home to complete the survey in the library before school. (If most of his students had not had access to e-mail accounts, he could have arranged for them to complete the survey in the school computer lab.) Mr. Solomon's survey is shown in Figures 1.7 and 1.8.

Mr. Solomon accesses the survey results online and tracks the answers as they are recorded. Back in class, he shares the survey results with his students and chooses the two most popular objectives as the focus of the week's lessons on the Battle of Leyte Gulf. He also allows his students to personalize some of their goals to reflect what aspects of the content are most important to them. As you can see from the results in Figure 1.9, the survey helps Mr. Solomon narrow the class objectives to "explain how the Japanese battle plan progressed and how the Americans reacted" and "explain why the Battle of Leyte Gulf was a major turning point in World War II." He'll address the other objectives in relation to these two main objectives.

The survey also helps Mr. Solomon identify student misconceptions to address before the class focuses on the main objectives. When he shares the survey results with the class, it elicits a vibrant discussion and debate about the significance of this particular battle. The survey results guide his lessons and assessments for the rest of the week.

Figure 1.7

Pre-assessment Survey Introduction Created with Survey Monkey

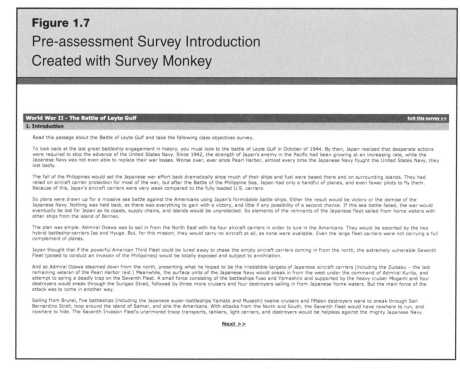

World War II - The Battle of Leyte Gulf   Exit this survey >>

1. Introduction

Read this passage about the Battle of Leyte Gulf and take the following class objectives survey.

To look back at the last great battleship engagement in history, you must look to the battle of Leyte Gulf in October of 1944. By then, Japan realized that desperate actions were required to stop the advance of the United States Navy. Since 1942, the strength of Japan's enemy in the Pacific had been growing at an increasing rate, while the Japanese Navy was not even able to replace their war losses. Worse over, ever since Pearl Harbor, almost every time the Japanese Navy fought the United States Navy, they lost badly.

The fall of the Philippines would set the Japanese war effort back dramatically since much of their ships and fuel were based there and on surrounding islands. They had relied on aircraft carrier protection for most of the war, but after the Battle of the Philippine Sea, Japan had only a handful of planes, and even fewer pilots to fly them. Because of this, Japan's aircraft carriers were very weak compared to the fully loaded U.S. carriers.

So plans were drawn up for a massive sea battle against the Americans using Japan's formidable battle ships. Either the result would be victory or the demise of the Japanese Navy. Nothing was held back, as there was everything to gain with a victory, and little if any possibility of a second chance. If this sea battle failed, the war would eventually be lost for Japan as its coasts, supply chains, and islands would be unprotected. So elements of the remnants of the Japanese fleet sailed from home waters with other ships from the island of Borneo.

The plan was simple. Admiral Ozawa was to sail in from the North East with his four aircraft carriers in order to lure in the Americans. They would be escorted by the two hybrid battleship-carriers Ise and Hyuga. But, for this mission, they would carry no aircraft at all, as none were available. Even the large fleet carriers were not carrying a full complement of planes.

Japan thought that if the powerful American Third Fleet could be lured away to chase the empty aircraft carriers coming in from the north, the extremely vulnerable Seventh Fleet (poised to conduct an invasion of the Philippines) would be totally exposed and subject to annihilation.

And so Admiral Ozawa steamed down from the north, presenting what he hoped to be the irresistible targets of Japanese aircraft carriers (including the Zuikaku – the last remaining veteran of the Pearl Harbor raid.) Meanwhile, the surface units of the Japanese Navy would sneak in from the west under the command of Admiral Kurita, and attempt to spring a deadly trap on the Seventh Fleet. A small force consisting of the battleships Fuso and Yamashiro and supported by the heavy cruiser Mogami and four destroyers would sneak through the Surigao Strait, followed by three more cruisers and four destroyers sailing in from Japanese home waters. But the main force of the attack was to come in another way.

Sailing from Brunei, five battleships (including the Japanese super-battleships Yamato and Musashi) twelve cruisers and fifteen destroyers were to sneak through San Bernardino Strait, loop around the island of Samar, and sink the Americans. With attacks from the North and South, the Seventh Fleet would have nowhere to run, and nowhere to hide. The Seventh Invasion Fleet's unarmored troop transports, tankers, light carriers, and destroyers would be helpless against the mighty Japanese Navy.

Next >>

Reproduced courtesy of SurveyMonkey.com.

Figure 1.8

Pre-assessment Survey Created with Survey Monkey

World War II - The Battle of Leyte Gulf   Exit this survey >>

2. The Battle of Leyte Gulf

1. What do you know about the results of the Battle of Leyte Gulf?

* 2. Which of the following learning objectives is most important to you?
- Understand how the Battle of Leyte Gulf fit into the overall Japanese strategy in the Pacific.
- Describe the major leaders and the effects of their decisions in the Battle of Leyte Gulf.
- Explain how the Japanese battle plan progressed and how the Americans reacted.
- Explain why the Battle of Leyte Gulf was a major turning point in World War II.
- Describe the significance of the Battle of Leyte Gulf in relation to the American invasion of the Japanese held Philippine Islands.
- Other (please specify)

3. How important do you think the Battle of Leyte Gulf was to each nation's effort to win the war?

	Very Important	Important	Somewhat Important	Not Important
United States?	⊙	⊙	⊙	⊙
Japan?	⊙	⊙	⊙	⊙

<< Prev   Done >>

Reproduced courtesy of SurveyMonkey.com.

Figure 1.9
Pre-assessment Survey Results from Survey Monkey

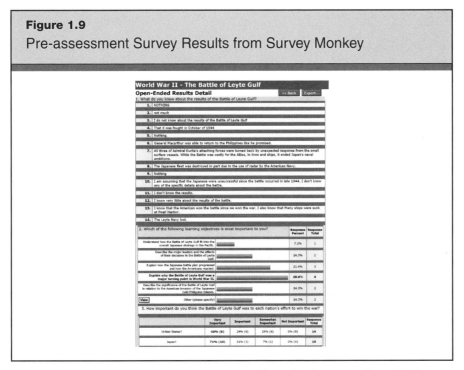

Reproduced courtesy of SurveyMonkey.com.

⟳ Web Resources

Teachers can use the vast resources of the Internet as a guide when setting objectives during the planning process. One way of applying Web resources to this end is to access standards online, transform them into objectives, and incorporate these objectives into a rubric that students can personalize.

As you are likely aware, your district, your state, and the United States as a whole have set standards in nearly every subject, and most teachers are required to tie these standards to their classroom objectives in some way. What are the steps teachers can follow to translate broad standards and benchmarks into rubrics to guide student learning? Start by looking up your school, district, or state standards. You might even use national standards, as they are the foundation of most state and district standards.

Here are three online sources for finding national education standards:

• McREL's Compendium of Standards: Content Knowledge
www.mcrel.org/standards-benchmarks

This online database of K–12 content standards and other valuable standards tools is used by district and state-level educators across the nation.

- Developing Educational Standards
http://edstandards.org/Standards.html

This site is a comprehensive list of standard sources by subject and region. It also includes many resources related to standards development, law, and professional organizations.

- Council of Chief State School Officers
www.ccsso.org/projects/State_Education_Indicators/Key_State_Education_Policies/3160.cfm

This site links to specific subject area standards by state departments of education.

Creating standards-based objectives. Let's say you are a middle school science teacher and that one of the standards in your curriculum is "Understands atmospheric processes and the water cycle." You might begin by going online to access McREL's Content Knowledge and finding the relevant benchmarks and indicators you will use to set the class and individual objectives (see Figure 1.10).

You decide that for this student project you will group some of the indicators into three objectives:

- *Objective 1:* Depict all of the water cycle patterns and processes in a clearly understandable and related fashion by researching the water cycle and creating a digital poster suitable for printing.
- *Objective 2:* Accurately describe five major processes in the water cycle and how they act as an interdependent cycle, using your poster as a visual aid.
- *Objective 3:* Correctly explain how the five major processes from Objective 2 affect climatic patterns, using your poster as a visual aid.

Creating rubrics. Now that you have set your objectives, how do you communicate them to your students? One answer: Create a rubric. Specific, criterion-referenced rubrics let students know exactly what is expected of them. However, rubrics like these are not always easy to design, and the process can eat up precious lesson

Figure 1.10
Excerpt from McREL's Content Knowledge

Science
Standard 1: Understands atmospheric pressure and the water cycle.

Topics 1. Water in the Earth system; 2. Seasons, weather, and climate
Level III (Grade 6–8)
Benchmark 2. Knows the processes involved in the water cycle (e.g., evaporation, condensation, precipitation, surface run-off, percolation) and their effects on climatic patterns.

Vocabulary terms
A. water cycle; B. evaporation in the water cycle; C. condensation in the water cycle; D. precipitation in the water cycle; E. surface run-off in the water cycle; F. percolation in the water cycle; G. climatic pattern.

Knowledge/skill statements
1. Knows the processes involved in the water cycle; 2. Knows the process of evaporation is part of the water cycle; 3. Knows the process of condensation is part of the water cycle; 4. Knows the process of precipitation is part of the water cycle; 5. Knows the process of surface run-off is part of the water cycle; 6. Knows the process of percolation is part of the water cycle; 7. Knows the effects of the water cycle on climatic patterns; 8. Knows the effects of condensation on climatic patterns; 9. Knows the effects of evaporation on climatic patterns; 10. Knows the effects of precipitation on climatic patterns; 11. Knows the effects of surface run-off on climatic patterns; 12. Knows the effects of percolation on climatic patterns.

planning time in a teacher's busy schedule. Fortunately, technology can make effective rubrics just a few clicks away.

A number of resources are available that help teachers and even students create rubrics. The following are a few of the Web sites dedicated to providing and designing rubrics. Explore these sites to create a multitude of rubric types.

• Rubrics for Web Lessons
http://edweb.sdsu.edu/webquest/rubrics/weblessons.htm

This site has a comprehensive discussion of rubric design for Web lessons and other topics. It also includes a generic rubric template and general guidelines.

• RubiStar
http://rubistar.4teachers.org/

This is a tool to help the teacher who wants to use rubrics but does not have the time to develop them from scratch. RubiStar provides generic rubrics that you can print and use for many typical lessons. It also provides these generic rubrics in a format that can be customized. You can change almost all suggested text in the rubric to make it fit your own objectives.

• Landmark Project Rubric Machine
www.landmark-project.com/rubric_builder/index.php

This "collaborative rubric toolkit" enables teachers to build effective assessment rubrics and to make them available over the Internet. Many teacher-designed rubrics are available.

• TeAchnology Web Portal for Educators
www.teach-nology.com/web_tools/rubrics

A number of well-designed rubrics are available for free on this site. After generating your rubric, you can select all, copy, and paste everything into a new word-processing document. Membership is not required to generate rubrics.

• Northwest Regional Education Laboratory: Science Inquiry Model
www.nwrel.org/msec/science_inq/guides.html

The rubrics available at this site (here, they are called scoring guides) help teachers assess students' performance of the essential traits of science inquiry: connecting, designing, investigating, and constructing meaning. The scoring guides define these traits and provide descriptive criteria for student performance, enabling teachers to give students precise and useful feedback as well as to inform their instructional objectives.

Ready to build a rubric from your learning objectives? Remember, the project objectives require the students to create and use a digital poster. For this example, go to RubiStar (http://rubistar.4teachers.org/), scroll down to the Create a Rubric section, and choose Products. Then choose Making a Poster to create a new rubric based on a template. Revise the Making a Poster rubric for a middle school project to research and create an accurate digital poster of the water cycle. Choose the criteria to fit the needs of your lesson, based on the objectives you created with your students. Notice that as you choose criteria, the rubric is automatically filled in for you. You can customize the text and add categories as you wish. Finally, choose Submit when you are ready to generate your rubric. The rubric maker will look something like Figure 1.11.

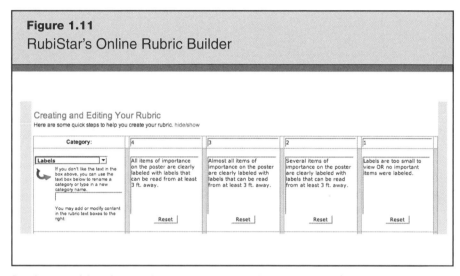

Figure 1.11
RubiStar's Online Rubric Builder

Development of this educational resource was supported, in part, by the U.S. Department of Education awards to ALTEC (Advanced Learning Technology in Education Consortia) at the University of Kansas Center for Research and Learning. These include Regional Technology in Education Consortium 1995–2005.

When you have completed all of the steps and have created your rubric, choose among saving the rubric online, printing it, or downloading it. The finished rubric will look something like the one in Figure 1.12. You might also guide students through this process so that they can customize rubrics for their own goals, based on the overall class objectives.

Now that you know how to create a custom, standards-based rubric, go back to RubiStar and look at the library of rubrics already available for use and modification. Click on the topic of your choice under the caption Create a Rubric from the menu (see Figure 1.13) to access an amazing number of rubrics.

○ Communication Software

Communication software, such as blogs (short for "Web logs") and e-mail applications, provide another way for you and your students to set and communicate goals and objectives.

Figure 1.12
Presentation Rubric Built with RubiStar

CATEGORY	4	3	2	1
Overall Concept and Pattern Description	Depicts all five of the major water cycle patterns and processes in a clearly understandable and related fashion	Depicts most of the major water cycle patterns and processes in an understandable and related fashion	Depicts some of the major water cycle patterns and processes in a somewhat understandable and related fashion	Depicts a few of the major water cycle patterns and processes in a confusing and unrelated fashion
Process and Cycle Description	Accurately describes all five major processes in the water cycle and how they act as an interdependent cycle, using the poster as a visual aid	Describes all five major processes in the water cycle and how they act as an interdependent cycle, using the poster as a visual aid	Describes most major processes in the water cycle, with some use of the poster as a visual aid	Describes few of the major processes in the water cycle, with little use of the poster as a visual aid
Explanation of Climatic Effects	Correctly explains how the five major processes in the water cycle affect climatic patterns, using the poster as a visual aid	Correctly explains how most of the five major processes in the water cycle affect climatic patterns, using the poster as a visual aid	Explains how some of the five major processes in the water cycle affect climatic patterns, with some use of the poster as a visual aid	Explains how a few of the five major processes in the water cycle affect climatic patterns, with little use of the poster as a visual aid
Graphics: Originality	Several of the graphics reflect an exceptional degree of student creativity in design and display	One or two of the graphics reflect an exceptional degree of student creativity in design and display	The student made the graphics, but the designs are based on the designs or ideas of others	There are no student-made graphics
Graphics: Relevance	All graphics relate to the topic and add to the presentation's impact; all borrowed graphics are accompanied by a source citation	All graphics relate to the topic; all borrowed graphics are accompanied by a source citation	Most graphics relate to the topic although some are superfluous; most borrowed graphics are accompanied by a source citation	Graphics do not relate to the topic OR several borrow graphics are not accompanied by a source citation

Blogs

A blog is a Web-based publication of periodic journal entries ("posts"), usually presented in reverse chronological order with the most current post appearing first. One way to think of a blog is as an online journal with one or many contributors. Because a blog is a personalized, dynamic Web page, it is much easier to maintain and design than a traditional, static Web page. Using a blog is similar to facilitating a focus group online.

Here's an example. Mrs. Birnbaum, a language arts teacher, wants to encourage reading during the upcoming winter break. She sets up a classroom blog and posts the titles and short, teaser-style descriptions of 10 short stories, along with possible learning objectives for each. Then she assigns the students to visit the blog site, read the posts, and choose three short stories to read over the two-and-a-half week break. After they read their three stories, they must comment on them, using one of the given learning objectives and another objective of their own. These posted comments show up as a threaded (chronological) discussion with other students who chose the same story. By the end of the winter break, Mrs. Birnbaum returns

Figure 1.13
RubiStar's Rubric Search

Find a Rubric
View, Edit, or Analyze a Rubric
Please enter your Saved Rubric ID below:

View | Edit | Analyze

Search for a Rubric
Choose your Search Type below:

⦿ Search Rubric **Titles**

○ Search Author **Name**

○ Search Author **Email Address**

Development of this educational resource was supported, in part, by the U.S. Department of Education awards to ALTEC at the University of Kansas Center for Research and Learning. These include Regional Technology in Education Consortium 1995–2005.

with information on each student's reading choices, objectives, and discussions. As you can see, this is not only a great tool for setting student objectives, it also is a wonderful way to differentiate student learning. Finally, when students return to the classroom, Mrs. Birnbaum facilitates the discussions of each story by first bringing up the online discussions from the blog. This gives students interesting information about the stories they did not read and makes it possible for them to post comments to the discussions of other stories.

There are many free online services available to guide you through the basic steps required to set up a blog. Most blog sites do not require you to download any software; they work through your Internet browser. Here is a list of the common features and capabilities that free blog services include:

- A variety of color and style templates to choose from
- Facilitator biography and information page link
- Response/read-level settings (e.g., public, class list, facilitator only)
- Comment-type settings (anonymous or by user name only)
- Comment on posts, or reply directly to other comments
- Delay, delete, or screen comments from users
- Facilitator and user pictures next to postings
- No banners or pop-up ads

If you are willing or able to pay a small fee, you will have access to more features, such as surveys and storage space; however, the free services are usually sufficient for classroom use.

Finally, the best way to understand how to use blogs to set objectives is to look at how other teachers use blogs with their classes. The Web site Teaching Blogs (http://escrapbooking.com/blogging/teaching.htm) provides hyperlinks to teacher blogs used as a tools for teaching and reflection, as well as for communicating with students, parents, or other teachers. We've listed some additional blog examples for you to browse. Many of the teachers who created them are just beginning to explore the full potential of using blogs with their students. As you delve into these example sites, think about ways you might use a blog with your own students.

- Ms. C's Geoblog
http://sculbreth1.edublogs.org

Student comments are encouraged in this high school geometry blog, used to keep students informed about class topics and assignments. Some assignments require students to post their answers to the blog itself.

- Mr. Mackey's Science Blog
http://mrmackeyscience.blogspot.com

This science class blog is linked to a comprehensive Web site used for all aspects of teaching 8th grade science. The blog is used to post current events, news, commentary, and useful links.

- Room 613 Talk: Mr. Hetherington's 6th Grade Social Studies Class
http://room613talk05.edublogs.org/about/

This is a class blog and podcast site for a 6th grade social studies class at Horace W. Porter School in Columbia, Connecticut. It is used to provide class information to students and the community. It also allows students to post essays and other assignments to the blog.

- Mr. Wright's 3rd Grade Class
www.mrwrightsclass.com

This comprehensive 3rd grade class blog from Wyman Elementary School in Rolla, Missouri, is used for all aspects of teaching elementary curriculum.

• Elizabeth Fullerton's English IV Weblog
www.elizabethfullerton.com/

This class blog at Columbia Central High School, Columbia, Tennessee, is used to teach senior English students writing, research, synthesis of ideas, and critical reading. Students are able to post and use the blog for collaborative writing.

E-mail

Written e-mail communication between a teacher and students is a simple way to set objectives in or out of school time. One aspect of setting objectives through e-mail is the ease in which the messages can be stored and recorded for future use in assessment and conferencing with students and parents. An e-mail newsletter is a second application of the technology and a clear alternative to traditional, hard-copy newsletters that students are supposed to take home and deliver. For example, you might collaborate with other teachers in your grade level, subject, or team and create a group newsletter to send to all parents on an e-mail distribution list. This newsletter might include a standard section that outlines the upcoming curricular topics and learning objectives for the class. Keeping parents informed about class learning objectives is one way to recognize them as the important team players that they are. It also helps parents keep their children focused on the right learning goals at home.

Here is an example of how one elementary grade-level team uses e-mail and newsletters to set objectives. At the beginning of the year, the 1st grade team collected all e-mail addresses available from parents. They found that about 92 percent of parents had an e-mail address they could access at home, work, or both. Now, the members of the team take turns editing a monthly 1st grade newsletter. The newsletter includes a message from the principal covering general school news and concerns, and it reports on events in special curriculum areas (music, art, physical education), along with news about clubs, sports, or other special subjects and activities.

The 1st grade teachers also post the electronic newsletter on their individual classroom blogs, and they print and post a hard copy on the classroom wall. They go over it with their students once a month on the day it is sent out to parents so that families can discuss it at home. The 1st grade team makes sure that all newsletters start out with the topics and a summary of the learning objectives for the upcoming month. The team has found that this has cut down on parent complaints and misinformation. In addition, they have noticed increased parental involvement since the team went to the e-mail newsletter system. The 8 percent of parents who do not use e-mail still rely on their children to deliver a hard copy to them, but each month, more and more parents are sending in their e-mail addresses and becoming part of the e-mail distribution system.

Before the 1st grade team started collaborating and sending newsletters by e-mail, parents often complained that they were confused by the multiple hard-copy newsletters coming home at different times from the music teacher, principal, teachers, and various committees. Furthermore, many students damaged or lost newsletters or simply forgot to give the newsletters to their parents. One teacher commented that she used be very frustrated to discover at teacher/parent conferences how little her students' parents knew about the learning objectives in her class. How could she ask parents to supervise homework, projects, and studying if they didn't even know what students were trying to learn? Now, more parents indicate that they receive and read the newsletter because it has all the information they need in one communication. They know when to expect the newsletter each month, and they no longer have to worry about students losing or damaging the newsletter before they see it. The class objectives are now easy to access. And as a final bonus, the time and money once invested in buying paper and arranging for bulk printing can be funneled into other activities.

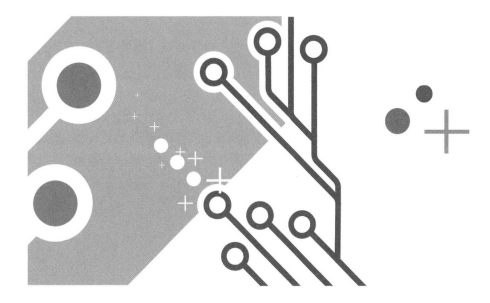

II. Which Strategies Will Provide Evidence of Student Learning?

Once you and your students have identified the skills and knowledge that they will learn, the next step is to decide how you will determine that students have indeed learned them: selecting the terms and means of obtaining evidence of mastery and giving feedback. Assessment can be *formative* (conducted during the learning process) or *summative* (conducted at the culmination of the unit or school year). It should comprise not only teacher-designed tests and projects, but also students' self-assessments, peer assessments, and automated assessments generated by hardware and software. Part II discusses the strategies teachers and students must use to generate this information—*providing feedback* (Chapter 2) and *providing recognition* (Chapter 3)—and the technologies that support these strategies.

2

PROVIDING FEEDBACK

The instructional strategy *providing feedback* focuses on formative assessment: giving students information about how well they are performing relative to a particular learning goal so that they can improve their practice. According to Harvard researcher John Hattie, who analyzed almost 8,000 studies on learning and instruction, feedback is "the most powerful single innovation that enhances achievement. The simplest prescription for improving education must be 'dollops' of feedback" (Hattie, 1992, p. 9).

McREL's research on providing feedback supports the following generalizations:

GENERALIZATIONS

1. Feedback should be corrective in nature.
2. Feedback should be timely.
3. Feedback should be specific to a criterion.
4. Students can effectively provide some of their own feedback.

Based on these generalizations, we have three recommendations for classroom practice:

RECOMMENDATIONS

1. Use criterion-referenced feedback.
2. Focus feedback on specific types of knowledge.
3. Use student-led feedback.

Research shows that the more immediate feedback is in classroom settings, the greater its impact on student behavior (Kulik & Kulik, 1988). Technology is especially effective when it comes to providing this kind of feedback. Games and simulations, for example, allow teachers and students to get near-instantaneous feedback *during* the learning process, allowing for immediate redirection or correction of misconceptions. Contrast this with holding feedback until the end of the lesson, unit, or school year. Technology also makes it easier to complete multiple reviewers' feedback on a student's work and allows the feedback process to happen ubiquitously.

In this chapter, we address the technology resources that facilitate and enhance the process of providing feedback for students and teachers: *word processing applications, data collection tools, Web resources,* and *communication software.*

○ Word Processing Applications

While many teachers and students use word processors as tools for writing, these programs also have features that support robust and timely feedback. In Microsoft Word, for instance, teachers and students can use the Track Changes and Insert Comments features to give and gather student-led feedback, which is one of the recommendations for classroom practice.

In Figure 2.1's illustration, you can see the feedback that Karen, a student writer, received from two different peer reviewers; the software displays each reviewer's comments in a different color. These comments can serve as the starting point for editorial decisions. Karen, for example, might accept some of the suggestions and reject others.

To track changes in Microsoft Word, be sure the Reviewing toolbar is visible. If it's not, go to View > Toolbars and select Reviewing. (The Track Changes icon looks like a piece of paper with red lines, a pencil, and a yellow star.) To insert a comment, go to Insert > Comment.

Figure 2.1
Microsoft Word Document Showing
Tracked Changes and Inserted Comments

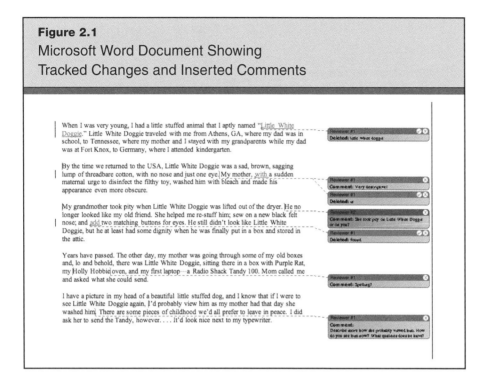

Saving documents in a group shared folder provides a way for an entire classroom of students to quickly access one another's work, and give and receive feedback from their teacher and their peers.

Another useful tool available in Microsoft Word is the Flesch-Kincaid Readability Scale, which calculates the complexity of a piece of writing in terms of sentence length and the number of syllables in the words used. When the tool is activated, every time a student runs a spell check, the software will display summary information and assign "reading ease" and grade-level ratings to the text. Although initially, students who take advantage of this tool might be interested mostly in their ratings, they can learn to use it to gather feedback on the sophistication of their writing. This follows the second classroom recommendation—to provide feedback on specific types of knowledge relevant to the subject matter. Figure 2.2 shows the Flesch-Kincaid Readability assessment of Karen's essay.

To use this feature, go to the Tools menu and select Options, and then click on the Spelling & Grammar tab. Click on the checkboxes for Check grammar with spelling and Show readability statistics.

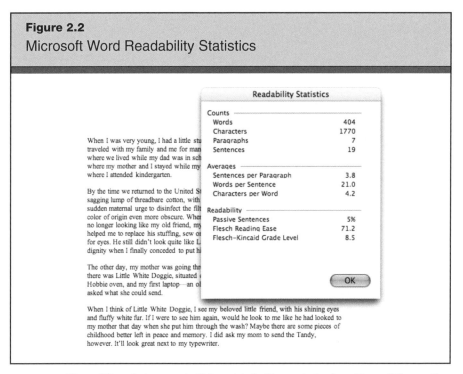

Figure 2.2
Microsoft Word Readability Statistics

Microsoft® product screen shot(s) reprinted with permission from Microsoft Corporation.

Once students know the readability scale level of a piece of writing, they can revise it before turning it in, paying close attention to word choice and variation. (You might also encourage students to use the built-in thesaurus in Word or www.visualthesaurus.com to refine their word usage.) After Karen addressed the some of the peer- and teacher-suggested changes and comments in her original essay (which, as the figure shows, rated an 8.5 on the Flesch-Kincaid Grade Level scale), the final version's score rose to 9.0. It's easy to see how this feature might help students approach the feedback and revision process as an engaging, game-like challenge.

○ Data Collection Tools

A frustration of being one teacher responsible for the learning of many students is that it can be tremendously difficult to provide each of them with specific and immediate feedback. Data collection tools are a wonderful help here. Remember that one of the generalizations from the research is that feedback should be timely. With data collections tools, it can be immediate.

Classroom Response Systems

Automated classroom response systems—also known as *student response systems*—provide teachers with a new way to gather and disseminate specific feedback. This tool collects data through the use of "clickers," then generates an immediate analysis of how students responded. Manufacturers of popular classroom response systems include eInstruction, EduGame, Promethean, and ClassAct. The screen shots included in this section are from eInstruction.

Classroom response systems rely on multiple-choice questions. Although it's common to think of multiple-choice questions as appropriate only when evaluating students' grasp of simple facts and vocabulary, when multiple-choice questions are appropriately designed, they can evaluate all levels of skill within Bloom's taxonomy, from recall through evaluation.

Consider this example: Mr. Faulk, a 2nd grade teacher, is using the eInstruction software to create a quiz that will check his students' understanding of animal classification. For his first formative assessment in the unit, he enters these questions into the system database:

1. Animals with backbones are called _____.
2. Animals without backbones are called _____.
3. Which of these animals is a vertebrate?
4. Which of these animals is an invertebrate?
5. Which of these is *not* a class of vertebrates?
6. Members of this class of vertebrates breathe with gills their entire life and lay eggs.
7. Members of this class of vertebrates spend part of their lives in water and part on land. They lay eggs.
8. Members of this class of vertebrates spend most of their time on land. Almost all lay eggs, but a few give live birth. They breathe with lungs. They are cold-blooded.
9. Members of this class of vertebrates are warm-blooded. They lay eggs, breathe with lungs, and are covered with feathers.
10. Which of these is not a characteristic of mammals?
11. A mouse is an example of _____.
12. A gecko is an example of _____.
13. A whale is an example of _____.

Notice that the numbered questions progress from basic, recall-level tasks to those requiring more comprehension and analysis of the basic facts and vocabulary of vertebrate classification. For each of these questions, Mr. Faulk is able to insert a range of answer options.

To facilitate comprehension for his emerging readers, he also may choose to substitute images or pictures for words in both questions and answers. The pictures in Figure 2.3's example come from www.clipart.com.

Figure 2.3
Design View of eInstruction with Pictures

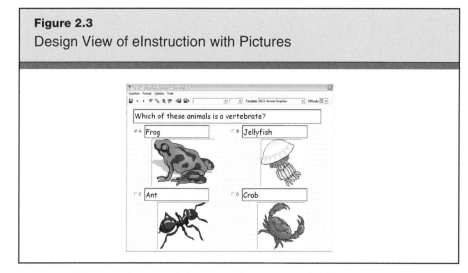

Reproduced courtesy of eInstruction. Clip art images © 2007 Jupiterimages Corporation.

Before Mr. Faulk administers the quiz he created, he gives each student a wireless clicker and explains that they will respond to each question within a set amount of time. Then he reads each question and prompts them to use their clicker to enter a response. The perceived anonymity of the responses makes for more honest answers and thus more accurate assessment; students are neither deterred by the fear of "looking stupid" in front of their peers nor swayed by the answers of others. When the response time is up, the feedback to students is immediate and specific. They can see from question to question whether they are answering correctly or not. At the end of the quiz, Mr. Faulk has many reports available to him. One is an Instructor Summary (see Figure 2.4), which shows each student's name and the percentage of questions that he or she answered correctly.

He also might choose to create a Question Report (see Figure 2.5) to see if particular questions posed problems for the class in general. In this example, a disproportionately large number of students

Figure 2.4
Instructor Summary from eInstruction

Instructor Summary

Session: Animal Classification
Class: Second Grade
Class Points Avg: 56.19 out of 100.00 (56.19%)
(Includes only students who took assessment)

Lesson

Pad ID	Student Name	Student ID	Correct/ Attempted	% Correct
1	01, Student		7 of 13	47% (15)
2	02, Student		4 of 13	27% (15)
3	03, Student		9 of 15	60% (15)
4	04, Student		6 of 14	40% (15)
5	05, Student		8 of 13	53% (15)
11	11, Student		13 of 14	87% (15)
22	22, Student		12 of 14	80% (15)

Reproduced courtesy of eInstruction.

Figure 2.5
Question Report from eInstruction

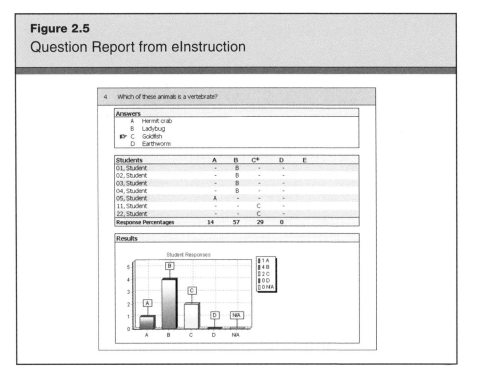

Reproduced courtesy of eInstruction.

responded that they thought a ladybug, rather than a goldfish, was an example of a vertebrate. These data are excellent feedback for Mr. Faulk, indicating that he needs to revisit this section of the animal classification lesson and address his students' misconceptions.

Finally, the teacher can print out a Study Guide for each student, showing which questions were answered correctly and giving the correct answer for those answered incorrectly (see Figure 2.6). Using this tool, teachers and students have access to a variety of data that give them instant feedback on student understanding of the material.

Figure 2.6
Study Guide from eInstruction

01, Student

Pad ID: 1
Student ID:

You answered 7 of 15 questions correctly for a percentage of 47%.

1 Animals with backbones are called ________.

A Fish
B Invertebrates
C Mammals
☞ D Vertebrates

You answered D.

✗ 2 Animals without backbones are called ______.

A Insects
☞ B Invertebrates
C Squishy
D Vertebrates

You answered C.

Reproduced courtesy of eInstruction.

Later in their study of animal classification, Mr. Faulk will pose more in-depth questions in order to assess if his students are able to synthesize or evaluate the information. Examples of higher-order questions include the following:

1. Imagine that, during a walk through a desert climate, you come across an animal that you have never seen before. You know from its body

shape—eyes that sit high on its head—and its skin texture that it is either a reptile or an amphibian, but you're not sure which. Without endangering yourself or the animal, how would you go about finding out which it is?

   a. Ask a local if there are any nearby streams or lakes, now or at some-time in the year.
   b. Touch the animal to see if the skin is moist and smooth or dry and scaly or bumpy.
   c. Watch to see what it eats.

2. The scientific theory of evolution claims that life started as simple organisms living in oceans and ponds. Based on this theory, which of these claims can you assume is correct?

   d. Everything living in the ocean evolved before everything living on land.
   e. Land dwellers are more complex that ocean dwellers.
   f. Reptiles evolved after amphibians because they have the ability to breathe on land.

With this batch of questions, Mr. Faulk will ask his students to share their thoughts with a partner before clicking the answer; this pair work is a way to elevate the level of classroom discussion and synergy of learning. We also encourage teachers to use classroom response systems in this way to start discussions with students, inviting individuals to defend their answers. Doing so gives students the benefit of answering anonymously and the chance to learn from debate and discussion in the classroom.

Grading Software

Manufacturers continue to develop more and more sophisticated grading software for use at all grade levels. In universities, some of the newest tools are capable of evaluating student essays and other larger projects, a process once believed to be something only humans could do. Makers of this type of software include Vantage Learning, Maplesoft, Educational Testing Service, and SAGrader. Studies thus far show a strong correlation between computer-generated scores and those of human experts (Adam, 2001). In one documented case, teachers found that using Vantage Learning's MY Access! software in their classes led to an improvement in student writing and an increase in how much time students devoted to the writing process ("High Schools Plug into Online Writing Program," 2003). If computer-assisted testing becomes the norm in universities, we can assume that K–12 classrooms will eventually adopt this practice as well.

○ Web Resources

Because we cover rubrics extensively in Chapter 1's discussion of setting objectives (see pages 17–33), we will not go into as much detail here, but we cannot overemphasize the wisdom of using rubrics to provide feedback on student attainment of the objectives set. Because rubrics provide detailed descriptions, they help teachers meet the classroom recommendation of giving feedback that's specific to a criterion as opposed to giving a simple grade or score. We also encourage the use of rubrics for peer evaluation. As students learn to work collaboratively, they need scaffolding in how to provide feedback in a specific, constructive, and supportive manner. Using a Web-based rubric creator, such as David Warlick's Landmark Project Rubric Builder (http://landmark-project.com/classweb/tools/rubric_builder.php), can help them to do that.

In this section, we focus on Web resources that present online quizzes, games, and simulations to provide immediate feedback. Educators and parents sometimes express concern about the role that games have in education, but we suspect they do so because they have an erroneous sense that "games in the classroom" means students zoned-out in front of a computer or TV screen. If the games and simulations are carefully chosen, they can be both educational and entertaining, and anything but mindless. Remember that doctors, soldiers, pilots, and even customer-service agents use simulations and games for training. In fact, a number of research studies suggest that bringing games and simulations into the K–12 classroom positively affects student motivation, retention, transfer, and skill level (Halverson, 2005; Klopfer, 2005; Prensky, 2000; Squire, 2001). And many educational and entertainment games encourage 21st-century skills such as solving problems, collaborating with other players, and planning (Klopfer, 2005). Another great characteristic of computers as "instructors" is that they are nonjudgmental entities. A struggling student can practice a skill as many times as necessary to achieve mastery, and the computer, unlike a human instructor, will never grow frustrated.

The best Web resources for games and simulations not only provide the student with judgment-free practice and immediate feedback but also make the activity fun. One such resource is iKnowthat.com (www.iknowthat.com). This site is designed for preK through 6th grade and has learning games for the arts, language arts, mathematics, science, social studies, and thinking skills. Each subject area has activities that are differentiated by grade level, and a teacher guide lists the standards that each activity addresses. To see an example, go to the Web site and navigate to Math > Leon's Math Dojo > Play. In this game, students choose an activity, which might range from basic counting practice to addition, subtraction, multiplication, and division. Taking on the role of Leon the Chameleon, a martial arts student dressed in a gi, students answer a series of questions by "kicking" the hanging bag displaying the correct answer to each. They receive visual and aural feedback as they play. If Leon selects an incorrect answer, the hanging bag flies backward and bonks him in the head. A "ding" signifies a correct response and triggers a new problem. This game is timed and displays a running tally of the number of questions attempted and the number of correct answers. Students can work to beat their best scores and those of their classmates.

Here is a sampling of other Web resources for games and simulations:

- Math Playground
www.mathplayground.com/index.html

This action-packed site for K–6 students provides engaging games that encourage students to challenge themselves.

- ExploreLearning
www.explorelearning.com

This Web resource is for middle and high school students and teachers. ExploreLearning allows students to use "gizmos"—virtual manipulatives—to experiment in science and mathematics. After going through a guided tutorial using the gizmos, the students take a short quiz. Their answers are assessed and they receive detailed feedback. Although ExploreLearning is a subscription site, a free 30-day pass is available upon sign-up. ExploreLearning's research shows that computer-based simulations are the ideal medium for conveying information in math and science (Cholmsky, 2003).

- Cut The Knot
www.cut-the-knot.org/games.shtml

This site is for teachers, parents, and students who seek engaging mathematics. It's a repository of nearly 700 applets that illustrate mathematical concepts. An applet is a software component that runs in the context of another program—a Web browser, for example. An applet usually performs a very narrow function, and it will run on any computer's browser.

Other Web resources provide information in a multimedia format and then quiz students on basic comprehension of the material. Although we discuss these types of resources in more detail in other sections of this book, there are two that warrant mention here due to the rich and immediate feedback that they provide students:

- BrainPOP
www.brainpop.com

This subscription-based resource has short Flash movies on a wide variety of topics in science, social studies, mathematics, English, health, and technology. The movies use clear animation to demonstrate concepts and highlight new vocabulary. After watching a movie, students can take a brief quiz and e-mail the results to their teacher, or they can rewatch the movie and retake the quiz as many times as they need to do so. BrainPOP also features some free movies and a free trial.

- BBC Skillswise
www.bbc.co.uk/skillswise

This Web site provides fact sheets, interactive applets, games, and quizzes in mathematics and language skills for grades K–6. Each quiz is broken into three levels so that students can advance as they learn the skill. This is especially helpful for teachers looking to provide differentiated instruction and assessment.

○ Communication Software

Communication software, such as blogs, wikis, e-mail, instant messaging (IM), and video conferencing, can provide timely, interactive, and criterion-based feedback to students. Each of these types of software has distinct classroom applications. For example, classroom blogs are inexpensive and easy to maintain and manage without the need for Web development skills. Wikis are similar to blogs but more versatile: a way for groups to collaborate by contributing and easily accessing information on a given topic. Because a wiki allows all users to add and edit content, it's especially suited for collaborative writing and project-based learning. The constant feedback mechanism of a wiki is what makes it a uniquely powerful learning tool. And because a wiki is Web-based, contributors do not need to be in the same geographical area, nor do they need to be working synchronously. Next, there's e-mail, which provides a written record of two-way communication that is easy to archive. Finally, while video conferencing has been used mostly for distance learning and teacher professional development, its use in K–12 education is growing. Because video conferences allow two or more locations to interact via two-way video and audio transmissions simultaneously, they serve to connect rural communities, distant classrooms, and experts with learning sources and classes from around the world.

Let's take a closer look at each of these types of communication software.

Blogs

A blog, short for "Web log," is a Web site in which items are posted on a regular basis and usually displayed in reverse chronological order. Like other media, blogs often focus on a particular subject, such as education, technology, or politics. However, blogs differ from other types of Web sites in that moderators frame the discussions and then invite readers to reply to posts. This works best in a written format, although blogs have the additional capability to display graphics and even video. The manager or facilitator of a blog can decide if others will be allowed to comment on postings to the blog.

If you want your classroom blog to be interactive, allowing student input and feedback, you will need to enable this comments feature. You can do this by allowing only certain registered users (your students) to post and blocking all others. Alternatively, you may set up your classroom blog to be open to postings from anyone. Remember, though, that blogs open to public postings sometimes receive inappropriate comments from unaccountable sources (online vandalism).

We recommend that teachers decide which students will be allowed to post to the classroom blog and make sure they understand the acceptable use policy in your school or district. Often, losing the privilege to comment to the class blog is consequence enough to keep students from posting inappropriate or offensive comments. Furthermore, as the manager of the blog, you can screen student comments before you allow them to be posted. Inappropriate blog postings are not as big a problem as you might think, provided that you stipulate students use their actual names as their user names; most students do not want their name on an offensive posting for all the school and their parents to see.

One example of providing feedback with a blog is a poetry journal blog. Ms. Jeargen, a middle school English teacher, posts a prompt on the class blog for students to write and post poems. As a follow-up, Ms. Jeargen posts a poetry rubric to the blog, reviews the rubric in class, and directs the students to review their classmates' poems and use the rubric to provide criterion-based feedback on three poems. In this way, students are exposed to other poems and both give and receive timely and meaningful feedback. Ms. Jeargen then closes the assignment thread from further student comments and provides her own criterion-based feedback as the last comment for each poem. Next, she starts a discussion that prompts the students to write their final draft of the poem. This thread is closed to comments. It will be used as the final product and can be viewed by other classes, parents, and the community. The various steps in the assignment are depicted in the project flow chart in Figure 2.7.

Wikis

Although we discuss wikis further when we look at technology that supports cooperative learning (see Chapter 7), we mention them here because users can give unlimited input and editing to each other using wikis to form a continually evolving body of knowledge. An

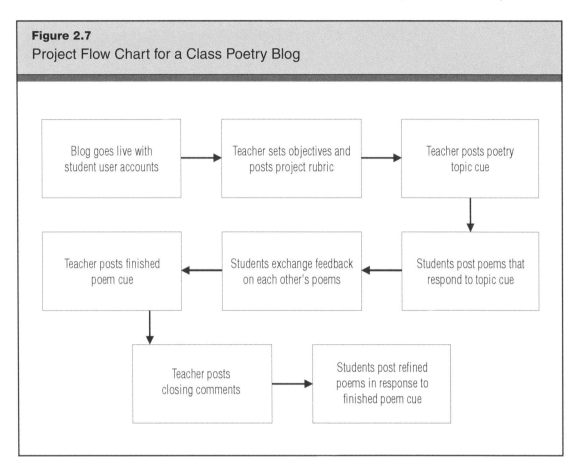

Figure 2.7
Project Flow Chart for a Class Poetry Blog

example is when students use a wiki to create a group project on a complicated subject, such as the civil rights movement. The teacher, and anyone else for that matter, sees exactly which students are contributing and how the group's combined input strengthens the final project.

Online, you can find various examples of how wikis are being used in many different subject areas. As with any resource, we encourage teachers to teach their students to gather information from a variety of sources. Teachers and students also need to understand that because anyone can make an entry on a wiki (like Wikipedia, for example), the information they find there must be viewed as one of several data points. Here are some recommended resources for wikis:

• High School Online Collaborative Writing
http://schools.wikicities.com

This Web site provides free wiki software that runs through your browser. You can set up a collaborative writing project on almost any subject as long as you do not violate the site's license agreement.

- Wikispaces
www.wikispaces.com

Wikispaces is a place for people to easily build Web pages together. Anyone can join the site for free, create a space, and begin contributing within a matter of minutes.

- Peanut Butter Wiki
http://pbwiki.com

This is a user-friendly and free wiki service site. Whether you make your wiki public or private, you choose a password that others must enter before they will be permitted to edit an entry.

E-mail

Teachers can send feedback to students through e-mail any time, whether in or out of school. Even students without home computer access can set up a Web-based e-mail account through a number of free services such as Gmail, Yahoo! mail, Hotmail, and Lycos that they can access through a classroom or library computer.

Consider the example of Mr. Dunlap, a high school civics teacher who wants to keep his class on track over the three-day weekend that marks the President's Day holiday. He sets a Friday deadline for a short essay assignment about the executive branch of government and asks students to submit their essays to him via e-mail, as attached Microsoft Word documents. Mr. Dunlap grades the essays at his leisure, then e-mails the graded essays back to the students on Sunday afternoon. Students receive this feedback in the form of the tracked changes and also in comments that he makes about the essays in his e-mail message. If a particular student's essay suggests that the student doesn't fully understand the assignment, Mr. Dunlap attaches the rubric for the essay. He can easily copy parents in this correspondence, and the e-mail software maintains a record of these exchanges along with essay submission and return dates. In addition, all the files are electronic, meaning there are no stacks of papers to shuffle through. It's easy to see that using e-mail to provide feedback has the additional benefits of being efficient, timely, and specific.

Instant Messaging

Many schools have begun using the tremendous power of instant messaging to bring true experts into the classroom for curriculum-based conversations and feedback on student understanding. Simple and free programs like AIM and iChat allow two-way text conversations and even group conferencing without putting stress on a school's network. If your class is studying how the government works, for example, you might call or e-mail your state or national representative and ask for 20 minutes of a staff member's time to talk about their role in government. Your students should prepare questions in advance and provide those questions to the staff member. When it's time for the instant message conference, project your computer onto a screen, and the conference is on. How better to learn about the intricacies of how government works than by talking to someone involved in the actual process and getting their reactions to students' insights?

Another way to use instant messaging to provide student feedback is to establish a time every week that students know you will be online—say, Thursday evening from 7:00 to 8:00 p.m. This allows students to pop online and ask any clarifying questions as they are working on homework or projects.

Video Conferencing

Sometimes video conferencing is the ideal way to gain access to unique expertise, cultures, and locations. For example, Mrs. Valenza, a Spanish teacher, wants to give her students conversational experiences. She arranges a video conference with an English language class at the sister school in Spain. The students perform skits in Spanish and English during the video conference. Afterward, the teachers exchange feedback about the skits and the language usage for each class. They encourage their students to ask questions: the American students in Spanish, and the Spanish students in English. Both groups of students also use a blog to give feedback to one another, again using the other group's native language to create their posts. The American students receive valuable feedback from the teacher in

Spain via video conference and from the students in Spain via the project blog.

Garnering feedback from authentic audiences like these is a powerful motivator. Other types of authentic audiences students can access through educational technology include poetry clubs, research scientists, and historical societies. Teachers can find a number of free programs available online to help them set up a video conference. These include www.ivisit.com, www.paltalk.com, and www.ichat.com (Macintosh only).

3

PROVIDING RECOGNITION

As an instructional strategy, *providing recognition* means giving students rewards or praise for accomplishments related to the attainment of a goal. Unlike most of the strategies outlined in *Classroom Instruction That Works,* it speaks to the general affective development of students rather than to their specific academic development. Teachers who implement this strategy successfully use recognition to positively influence their students' attitudes and beliefs about accomplishment.

McREL's research on providing recognition supports the following generalizations:

GENERALIZATIONS

1. Rewards do not necessarily have a negative effect on intrinsic motivation.
2. Reward is most effective when it is contingent on the attainment of some standard of performance.
3. Abstract symbolic recognition (e.g., praise) is more effective than tangible rewards (e.g., candy, money).

Based on these findings, we have three recommendations for classroom practice:

RECOMMENDATIONS

1. Personalize recognition.
2. Use the Pause, Prompt, and Praise strategy.
3. Use concrete symbols of recognition.

One of the most powerful ways that technology facilitates the use of this strategy is that it gives teachers a way to expand recognition beyond giving a student an *A+* on an assigning or posting it on the classroom bulletin board. With technology, teachers can easily make exemplary work available for the appreciation of peers, parents, and professionals across the world. In *The Wisdom of Crowds,* James Surowiecki (2004) makes the similar argument that a large and diverse group working collectively makes better decisions and recognizes what's "best" better than a single individual can. Web sites such as Digg (www.digg.com) and Clipmarks (www.clipmarks.com) operate by this principle, allowing visitors to recognize which news items or Web clippings are most useful.

Technology tools can help teachers create personalized certificates or rewards and give individual, group, and class recognition through automated classroom response systems. In this chapter, we show how a teacher can use the following resources to provide recognition: *data collection tools, multimedia, Web resources,* and *communication software.*

○ Data Collection Tools

In Chapter 2's discussion of providing feedback, we described the use and capabilities of Web-based surveys and classroom response systems (see pages 45–58). Here, we offer two ways to use these same tools to provide recognition.

Because Web-based surveys and classroom response systems allow students to receive feedback from both teachers and peers, you can use these tools to recognize students who earn the highest-scoring feedback. When doing so, always remember to base recognition on a clear standard of performance. This is especially crucial with student recognition of their peers' work. Teacher-set parameters are the best way to ensure that the recognition reflects the standards-based criteria and not student popularity or another outside factor.

Here's an example of how a teacher might use data collection tools to provide recognition. Having just concluded a unit on the Great Depression, middle school students post original movies, essays, digital images of artwork, or other products to a designated Web site. On or before the assignment's due date, all students make their blog posts anonymously, using a teacher-assigned code instead of their actual names. Then, the students use a Web-based survey, such as Survey Monkey, to review a project rubric, view the posted products, and give rubric-based feedback, including a "grade." The program tallies the scores, after which the teacher reveals the names of the students whose products receive the highest scores, and they are formally recognized for completing high-quality work that meets the criteria described in the project rubric. This kind of personalization is in line with McREL's first classroom recommendation for providing recognition.

In another example, a mathematics teacher might give a pop quiz using a classroom response system, with the expectation that if the students' collective responses achieve an agreed-upon proficiency level, such as 90-percent accuracy, they will all earn bonus points to redeem later in the year. When the quiz is complete, the classroom response system returns an immediate verdict on the students' performance: They've earned their bonus points! The teacher gives the students verbal praise and distributes "bonus point coupons," following the classroom recommendation to provide concrete symbols of recognition. Note that in this example, the teacher rewards the entire class, encouraging students to help each other achieve. At other times, it might be appropriate to look at individual student response records and reward students individually.

⟳ Multimedia

Remember that one of the classroom recommendations from the research is to personalize recognition for your students, and another is to provide concrete symbols of recognition. Handing a student a personalized certificate to celebrate high-quality work is a way to do both and a surefire way to make that student feel appreciated and motivate further success. There are several software programs that make it easy for teachers to provide this kind of concrete recognition. For example, at http://office.microsoft.com/en-us/templates, you can download free templates for Microsoft Word and Microsoft Power-Point that make designing and printing certificates a snap.

In addition to this free resource, you might seek out software programs designed to create certificates, cards, banners and more. One of the best on the market is The Print Shop Deluxe, available from Broderbund. You can easily create a certificate or card with the student's name and even include a photo.

Figure 3.1 shows a certificate that a middle school principal awarded to a student who won first place in a school essay contest. The principal downloaded a template from the Microsoft site and edited it in Microsoft PowerPoint, personalizing the template to fit the specific occasion.

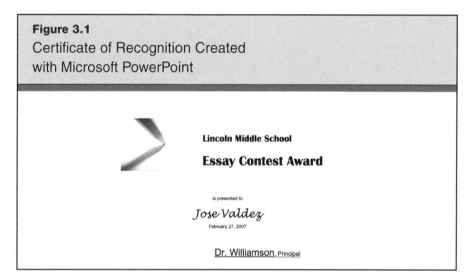

Figure 3.1
Certificate of Recognition Created with Microsoft PowerPoint

Lincoln Middle School

Essay Contest Award

Is presented to

Jose Valdez

February 27, 2007

Dr. Williamson, Principal

Clip art images © 2007 Jupiterimages Corporation.

○ Web Resources

McREL's meta-analysis shows that providing personalized recognition based on specific and individualized performance objectives is a powerful student motivator. In addition to the recognition you can provide with programs like Print Shop, you might explore many of the resources available on the Web, including online showcases or galleries of student work, online certificate/greeting card creators, and e-mailed voice messages.

Web Showcases and Picture Galleries

When a student brings home an example of outstanding schoolwork to show his or her parents, the parents often praise the child and post work on the household refrigerator for everyone in the home to see and admire. This is a good example of informally recognizing a student based on individual achievement. Technology provides a way to take this recognition to the next level. Posting exceptional student work on the Internet opens up possibilities for recognition from friends, peers, professionals, and relatives across the globe. Many of these Web sites stay up for years, providing examples to other students and becoming a lasting source of pride and confidence for the recognized students.

For instance, Reagan, a struggling 5th grade student, sets a goal with her teacher to write a three-page story about her favorite time of the year. She agrees to include proper writing conventions and to produce a paper that is free of grammatical errors. After working hard at drafting, revising, and editing, she accomplishes her goal. The teacher posts the story to the class's "Student Work Showcase" on the school's Web site and includes an annotation that recognizes the story as an accomplishment compared to the student's learning objectives. After the posting, Reagan telephones her grandparents in another state so they can see her work on their home computer.

Physical education and art teachers often use online picture galleries as a means of recognition because exhibitions are natural extensions of those content areas, but picture galleries are a fantastic way of motivating students and recognizing their efforts in any content area. Of course, always check your district's policy on the posting of student work. Also take care to post a diverse sampling of student work and not just products from the best and brightest students. When selecting work to post, assess how well a student has achieved his or her own goals for improvement rather than comparing the work to that of other students.

One example of a photo gallery service is the popular Flickr (www.flickr.com). Setting up a free account is simply a matter of providing a user name and a password. Once you have an account, you can upload pictures, enter comments, and send a link to the account Web page to students, parents, and colleagues. You can also restrict the page to only certain viewers or choose to make it available to the general public. If you add a few key word tags in your account profile, anyone will be able to find the page by searching Flickr.

Additional examples of providing recognition through Web showcases and picture galleries are available at the following Web sites:

- Mrs. McGowan's Student Showcase
www.mrsmcgowan.com/1stgrade/student_showcase.htm

This Web site is an excellent example of an elementary showcase site from H. W. Mountz Elementary School in Spring Lake, New Jersey. It highlights student work, Internet projects, class activities, and online resources for parents, children, and visitors.

- Greeneville Middle School—Celebrations
www.gcschools.net/gms/Recognitions/recognitions.htm

This award-winning Web site features student work and accomplishments at Greeneville Middle School in Greeneville, Tennessee.

- Kids' Space—Kids' Gallery
www.kids-space.org/index.html

This is a very large collection of international student work in all elementary school subjects. It's presented in multiple media: stories, artwork, and musical compositions.

- Kennedy High School Art Gallery
www.kenn.cr.k12.ia.us/ngallery/default.aspx

This fantastic collection of high school student art is from Cedar Rapids, Iowa, and includes animations, sculpture, photography, drawings, paintings, and digital art.

- Pleasantdale Elementary Physical Education Picture Gallery
www.pleasantdale.k12.il.us/elementary/pe/pe.htm

This is not the typical gallery of athletes holding up trophies, but an Illinois elementary school's collection of photographs highlighting student efforts in a standard physical education class.

- Apple Learning Interchange Student Gallery
http://edcommunity.apple.com/gallery/student/index.php

This digital media gallery allows students to create, post, and promote their work in the form of movies, animations, pictures, music, and presentations. Those with user accounts can choose their favorites for special recognition.

- New Technology High School Student Portfolios
www.nths.nvusd.k12.ca.us/School/Students_parents/portfolios.asp

All students at New Technology High School in Napa, California, are required to post student work portfolios. Follow the Recognition > Students link at the top of the page to find pictures of the "Students of the Month."

Online Certificates

Sending an online certificate of recognition is easy and often free. Some noteworthy examples of online certificate and greeting card services are listed here:

- Microsoft Office Education Resources
http://office.microsoft.com/en-us/templates/

This is a large collection of resources free for use with Microsoft Office software.

- Education Oasis
www.educationoasis.com/teacher_tools/Awards/awards_certificates.htm

Education Oasis is an independent, not-for-profit site where teachers can acquire ideas, information, and inspiration. Its stated goal is to provide quality materials that will help teachers take their practice to the next level.

- AAA Certificates
www.printablecertificateawards.com

This site offers many free award certificates printable from your Web browser.

- American Greetings E-Cards
www.americangreetings.com/ecards.pd

A site subscription is necessary before sending an e-card (although a 30-day free trial period is usually offered).

- Yahoo! Greetings
www.yahoo.americangreetings.com

This site has many free e-cards from which to choose.

In addition to posting student work and providing certificates for download, Web resources also include many online interactive games that provide recognition to students through the awarding of points, sounds, and audio messages (such as "Great job!"). Some games also offer hints and cues if a player does not answer or perform a virtual task correctly, encouraging the player to try again, and greet the new, correct response with fanfare. In this regard, they can help teachers follow the classroom recommendation of using the Pause, Prompt, and Praise strategy.

○ Communication Software

Today's communication software capitalizes on individuals' natural desires to socialize, to connect with one another, and to express opinions. In the modern classroom, e-mail and video conferencing present new ways for teachers to provide recognition to all learners.

Audio E-mail

Audio messages can be an unexpected and exciting way for students to receive recognition. Hearing the congratulatory tone and enthusiasm in a teacher's voice often leaves a lasting impression. Recording oral praise on a computer and sending the audio file as an e-mail attachment is easier than you might think. Many computer operating systems include a simple sound recorder program. On a computer running Microsoft Windows, it is usually found in the Entertainment folder, which is in the Accessories folder. On a Macintosh computer, you can record audio with iMovie or by upgrading to QuickTime Pro. You might also use many simple audio recording applications available for free download over the Internet. Audio files attached to e-mail are very small compared to most multimedia; the entire e-mail file will range between approximately 100 and 800 kilobits, depending on the length of the message.

Here's example of how a teacher might incorporate audio e-mail recognition. Mr. Webster, a high school geometry teacher, is grading a set of mathematics quizzes and finds that one of his students has made significant improvement in the ability to calculate and graph the slope of a linear equation. For a week, he has worked closely with this student, trying to ensure that she grasps the key concepts. He is so happy with her progress that he decides to send the student a simple audio recording praising her for meeting her goal to improve this skill. He simply opens his audio recording program on his computer, vocalizes his praise, saves the file, and sends her an e-mail greeting with the direction to open the attached audio file. She receives the audio message and is delighted to get the timely recognition.

Video Conferencing

Video conferencing allows two-way or multipoint communication in more personable, meaningful, and relevant ways than e-mail or telephone can provide. Through video conferencing, students can communicate with peers and have contact with professionals who can serve as authentic audiences for student work.

A thriving example of using video conferencing to provide recognition is the Global WRITeS project. (WRITeS is an acronym for Writers and Readers Incorporating Technology in Society). This nonprofit organization's mission is to promote literacy through the performing arts using technology resources such as video conferencing and digital media. Now in its ninth year, the project, based in the Bronx, New York, brings together performance poets, classroom teachers, and students to create integrated poetry units. As students write their poems, they practice performing them for students in other classrooms connected via room-based video conferencing. After the performances, they revise their writing, incorporating the feedback they receive from their peers. The poetry studies culminate twice per year in a video conference "slam session" of competitive performance poetry in which teams of five, chosen by peers as representatives of their schools, perform their pieces for the entire school district. Performances are judged by a panel of peer poets and two adults from the district's regional office. All of the teaching artists in the program come from an innovative arts-in-education organization, DreamYard, which partners with Global WRITeS to integrate arts programs into Bronx schools.

The students are involved in the development of every stage of the program, from making suggestions on "slam rules," to helping write the performance rubric, to serving as panel judges. The program is an integral part of the regular classroom day, facilitated during literacy block periods. At the time of this publication, 26 schools in the Bronx were participating. Currently, the program involves students in grades 3 through 8, but plans to expand into the upper grades are underway.

The project underwent a three-year, quasi-experimental study called Poetry Express, to determine its effectiveness. Funded by the U.S. Department of Education and conducted by METIS Associates, the study followed two elementary schools and two middle schools. Comparison schools with matching demographics provided the control group. Preliminary data demonstrated significant increases in student motivation and commitment to school as well as improvement on standardized tests, attendance, and writing quality. Students also developed collaboration skills and were able to have constructive, honest conversations about each other's work (Fico, 2005).

Technology plays a diverse and significant role in this example and models how effective video conferencing can be as a tool for providing recognition. Initially, students use blogs to publish and share written work with each other. Then they use video conferencing to engage in real conversations about their poetry, particularly during the writing and practice phase, where they give and receive feedback on performances. In a school district that is geographically spread out, such as the Bronx, it is costly and difficult to get students to the same physical location for this kind of regular collaboration. Video conferencing drastically reduces travel time, allowing more time for other subjects. All students get to see all performers, as well as the judges, during the slam sessions, and older students who have previously experienced the slam sessions mentor younger students. Perhaps most important, the students receive personalized feedback from peers and published performance poets. Through video conferencing, student writing is validated in face-to-face exchanges.

For additional resources related to the Global WRITeS project, visit one of the following Web sites:

- Global WRITeS
www.globalwrites.org

This is the official Web site for the Global WRITeS project. Users can find more information about the project, examples of student work, and research data.

- DreamYard
www.dreamyard.com/

DreamYard is an innovative arts-in-education organization that integrates the arts into the curricula of elementary, middle, and high school students. On this Web site, users can find out more information about DreamYard and about lesson plans and student artifacts.

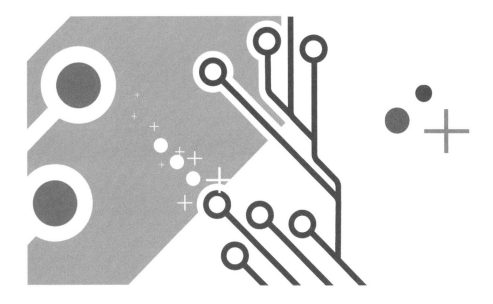

III. Which Strategies Will Help Students Acquire and Integrate Learning?

Guided by the first two planning questions, you have identified the learning objectives for your lesson and have selected the terms and means of assessing performance and giving feedback. Now you have the fun and interesting task of helping students acquire and integrate new knowledge. In order to do this, you need to help students activate their background knowledge and facilitate the process of connecting new information to what they already know so that they begin to see patterns and understand processes. Part III discuss the categories of instructional strategies that fall into this phase of the learning process: *cues, questions, and advance organizers* (Chapter 4); *nonlinguistic representation* (Chapter 5); *summarizing and note taking* (Chapter 6); *cooperative learning* (Chapter 7); and *reinforcing effort* (Chapter 8). Research shows that these strategies provide scaffolding for new information so that students have a higher chance of understanding and retaining the concepts.

4

CUES, QUESTIONS, AND ADVANCE ORGANIZERS

The instructional strategy *cues, questions, and advance organizers* focuses on enhancing students' ability to retrieve, use, and organize information about a topic.

In Chapter 1, we talked about using a KWL or KWHL chart to activate prior knowledge. To help students complete the "What do you know?" and "What do you want to know?" sections of this chart, teachers often use cues and questions. *Cues* are explicit reminders or hints about what students are about to experience. *Questions* perform the same function as cues by triggering students' memories and helping them to access prior knowledge. Advance organizers, a concept originally developed by David Ausubel (1960), are structures that teachers provide to students before a learning activity to help them classify and make sense of the content they'll encounter, particularly new content that is not well organized in its original format. In essence, advance organizers help students focus their learning.

McREL's research on cues, questions, and advance organizers supports the following generalizations:

GENERALIZATIONS

1. Cues, questions, and advance organizers should focus on what is important rather than what is unusual.
2. "Higher-level" questions and advance organizers produce deeper learning than "lower-level" questions and advance organizers.
3. Advance organizers are most useful with information that is not well organized.
4. Different types of advance organizers produce different results.
5. Waiting briefly before accepting responses from students has the effect of increasing the depth of students' answers.
6. Questions are effective learning tools even when asked before a learning experience.

Based on these findings, we have seven recommendations for classroom practice:

RECOMMENDATIONS

1. Use expository advance organizers.
2. Use narrative advance organizers.
3. Teach students skimming as a form of advance organizer.
4. Teach students how to use graphic advance organizers.
5. Use explicit cues.
6. Ask questions that elicit inferences.
7. Ask analytic questions.

Technology's potential applications are readily evident in this strategy, as teachers and students can use a variety of technology tools to create well-organized, visually appealing organizers. In this chapter, you will see what we mean, as we examine ways to use *word processing applications, spreadsheet applications, organizing and brainstorming software,* and *multimedia applications.*

We can recommend several resources that focus on the concept of "higher-level" or "essential" questions and provide excellent examples:

• From Trivial Pursuit to Essential Questions and Standards-Based Learning
www.fno.org/feb01/pl.html

This article by Jamie McKenzie looks at the differences between trivial, meaningless questions and those that truly encourage students to use critical thinking skills.

• Applying Bloom's Taxonomy
www.teachers.ash.org.au/researchskills/dalton.htm

This Web site goes through each level of Bloom's taxonomy and gives examples of questions, verbs, and potential activities for each level.

• Bloom's Taxonomy Model Questions and Key Words
www.utexas.edu/student/utlc/lrnres/handouts/1414.html

This resource from the University of Texas at Austin provides suggested cues and questions to use at each level in Bloom's taxonomy.

• For the Best Answers, Ask Tough Questions
www.joycevalenza.com/questions.html

This is an outstanding article on the topic of essential questions, written by Joyce Valenza and originally published in the April 2000 issue of the *Philadelphia Inquirer*. An essential question is one that requires the student to make a decision or create a plan. It requires more than simple research and regurgitation of answers. The article includes links to other resources addressing the topic of essential questions.

The technologies that support cues, questions, and advance organizers assist teachers in quickly capturing student responses and organizing the responses into useful information.

☼ Word Processing Applications

Word processing programs are extremely versatile and well suited as tools to create advance organizers, whether expository, narrative, or graphic. *Expository* advance organizers include brochures, definitions, rubrics, and programs. *Narrative* advance organizers are usually stories, articles, or artistic works. *Graphic* advance organizers are usually tables, charts, or artistic works.

Teachers can use expository, narrative, and graphic advance organizers alone or combine them to form compelling introductory materials that will help students focus on the essential concepts and themes that will prepare them to learn. For instance, if you are taking your students on a field trip, have them conduct research on the Internet beforehand and create a simple brochure using word processing software. The brochure might contain useful information that students can refer to during the trip, including maps, facts, and pictures. You might also have them copy and paste it into an agenda that you have created with a word processor and saved to your school's server or another commonly accessible location. Prior to embarking on the trip, students could skim the brochure as an additional advance organizer.

Another application of word processing programs is the use of table-making features to create an advance organizer for note taking. At the beginning of a lesson, the teacher gives students a two-column notes template with key terms, concepts, or themes for the day's instruction listed in the first column. As the lesson progresses, the students can gradually fill in this skeleton with explanatory text, Web links, and pictures. This helps students organize their thoughts around the essential information and gets them thinking about what they know about the topic even before the teacher has fully begun the lesson. This expository advance organizer could be posted for all to see on a computer projector or saved to a central server for the students to download. Furthermore, because the notes are digital, students can easily revise them and e-mail them home for study.

To create a note-taking template as a table in Word, click on Table > Insert > Table and enter the number of columns and rows you want the initial table to have. Don't worry if you misjudge the size of the table; you can easily insert or delete rows and columns later.

○ Spreadsheet Software

Although spreadsheet software may not be the first technology tool you think of when you want to create an advance organizer, it may actually be the best choice when a lesson is very unique or when you want to use spreadsheet functions in a rubric. Rubrics are excellent advance organizers because they prepare students to apply their abilities, knowledge, and critical thinking skills. Combining the expository information in a rubric with artistic narrative organizers is an effective strategy for preparing students to learn.

Here's an example. Mrs. Kedzierski, a high school language arts teacher, is planning a poetry writing lesson. For a narrative advance organizer, she gives students a selection of poems that set the mood for a major historical period: the Renaissance. The vocabulary, tone, and story line of poems by Shakespeare, Donne, and Jonson help activate students' prior knowledge and awaken their curiosity. After students read several of Shakespeare's sonnets, they write their own, as if they too were living in Elizabethan England. Of course, writing from this perspective is not easy and requires some up-front guidance. Mrs. Kedzierski decides to create a rubric to pass out to the students before they begin their writing.

Although Mrs. Kedzierski is familiar with online rubric-making sites, she prefers to create her own in Microsoft Excel or in a word processing program, using the table-making features. When using Excel, she first types her lesson criteria (e.g., *follows sonnet format, uses vocabulary appropriate to the time, sets story in Elizabethan period*) into the cells. Then she applies her desired formatting, colors, and fonts. She decides to program the spreadsheet to automatically tabulate the rubric score as she grades the poems. She does this by highlighting the cell under the rubric sub-scores column and choosing the f_x on the formula bar. Then she selects the SUM function and makes sure the summation selects the proper range of sub-scores, such as D1:D4. Now she has a rubric she can use quickly and easily over and over again.

○ Organizing and Brainstorming Software

One recommendation from the research is that teachers use explicit cues. By that, we mean your cues should be straightforward and provide students with a preview of what they are about to learn. Although it's common to think that cues should be subtle or ambiguous—like hints—in the classroom, a direct approach is most effective. Simply tell students what content they are about to learn.

For illustration, consider Ms. Douglas, a 6th grade science teacher who starts a unit on the physical properties of bridges by announcing to her students that they will be looking at different types of bridges, the parts of bridges, and why different bridges serve different purposes. She uses a Kidspiration organizer (see Figure 4.1) to show the class their learning goal. With the software, she has access to a vast database of visual aids, such as clip art and photographs of different types of bridges. As the lesson continues, Ms. Douglas and her students can add more cues and questions to the organizer in the form of both text and images.

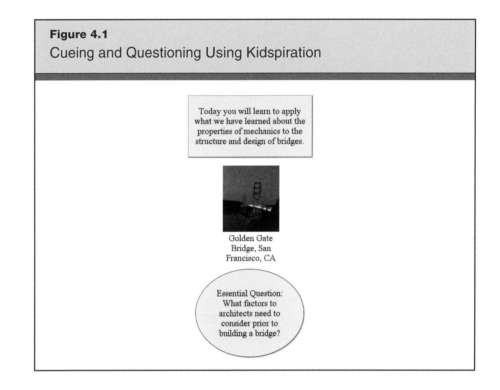

Figure 4.1

Cueing and Questioning Using Kidspiration

Today you will learn to apply what we have learned about the properties of mechanics to the structure and design of bridges.

Golden Gate Bridge, San Francisco, CA

Essential Question: What factors to architects need to consider prior to building a bridge?

Notice that Ms. Douglas has also included an *essential question* in this Kidspiration organizer. Asking students to use background knowledge to answer essential questions aligns with research showing that higher-order questions produce deeper learning than lower-order questions do (Marzano, Pickering, & Pollock, 2001). In this example, the essential question is intended to elicit inferences from the students, as it is not information that will be specifically stated to them. Later in the unit, Ms. Douglas could ask her students, "If you were hired to correct problems with the Tacoma Narrows Bridge prior to its demise, what advice would you give to the builders?" In this case, Ms. Douglas is asking her students to analyze and critique something using the knowledge that they've learned about bridges, thereby meeting the seventh and final classroom recommendation for using cues, questions, and advance organizers: asking analytic questions.

To begin this lesson on bridges, the teacher has her students fill in a KWL chart to activate their background knowledge. Because they are doing this activity in conjunction with their study of forces of motion, Ms. Douglas gives explicit cues that will help students connect the content. She states, "As you think about your answer to the essential question of which factors architects need to consider before building a bridge, also think about Newton's Third Law of Motion: that for every action, there is an equal and opposite reaction." As a final cue, she could use multimedia to activate background knowledge by showing a selected movie or activity, such as those available from ExploreLearning, BrainPOP, United Streaming, or PBS. While some of these resources are subscription-based, most allow either a free trial period or limited free access. (We discuss multimedia and advance organizers later in this chapter.)

As a teacher, when you provide cues and questions like ones Ms. Douglas provides, students have a clearer sense of what they are going to learn. To aid the learning process, look for opportunities to activate students' background knowledge, thereby providing a direction for exploration. The technology, in turn, provides you with editable visual aids and multimedia resources that appeal to a number of learning styles. Auditory learners have the added benefit of being able to listen many times to information in order to understand it better. Visual learners use the pictures and video as visual clues to understanding the content. The motion portrayed in the video can reach kinesthetic learners by helping them to picture the motion of forces associated with bridges.

Let's take a look at how Ms. Douglas might use the same software to create an advance organizer to further her 6th graders' study of bridges. Kidspiration and Inspiration software are ideal tools for creating advance organizers, and specifically graphic organizers. Whether these organizers are used digitally with students or printed out for them to complete by hand, organizing and brainstorming software allows learners to add and organize information as it is being introduced.

Ms. Douglas's goal is to get her students to apply the concepts they learned during a study of Newton's Laws of Motion to real-world purposes. Particularly, she wants to have them learn about different types of bridges and how engineers decide which type of bridge to build in various situations. She uses Inspiration to create an advance organizer. It includes blank areas to label the types of bridges and the forces acting upon them. She leaves blank sections and instructs her students to fill these in with a drawing of each type of bridge, complete with arrows showing the stresses. She also includes a word bank to introduce new vocabulary terms.

Next, Ms. Douglas incorporates multimedia into this process of cueing and questioning. She provides her students with a collection of links to online multimedia resources, where they can find the information they'll need to complete the advance organizer:

• **How Bridges Work** (http://science.howstuffworks.com/bridge.htm). This Web site offers detailed explanations of how things work. The articles are broken into chapters, and vocabulary terms are in bold.

• **PBS Building Big: Bridges** (www.pbs.org/wgbh/buildingbig/bridge/index.html). This series of tutorials offers applets and short games to introduce the physics behind bridges, domes, skyscrapers, dams, and tunnels.

• **NOVA Online: Super Bridge** (www.pbs.org/wgbh/nova/bridge/). This simulation has students learn about different types of bridges and then apply their skills by deciding which bridge type will work best in various situations.

• **BrainPOP** (www.brainpop.com/technology/scienceandindustry/bridges/). This short movie introduces basic vocabulary and concepts behind bridges.

As the students are introduced to new vocabulary terms and concepts, they fill in the blank sections. Figure 4.2 shows one student's completed organizer.

Later, as the students delve deeper into the concepts, the teacher can add to this organizer. The word bank can grow as the students learn more vocabulary. If she chooses, Ms. Douglas can even use this organizer as a final assessment piece by giving students a blank graphic organizer at the end of a unit and asking them fill-in the text and drawings.

Figure 4.2

Completed Advance Organizer Created in Inspiration

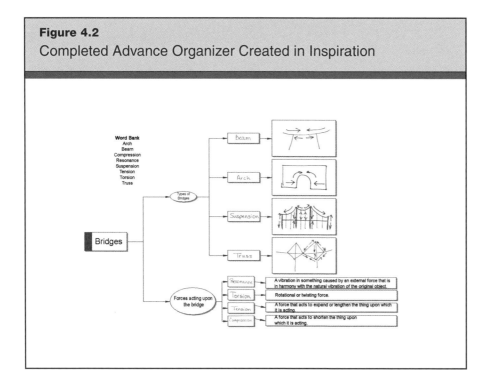

Let's look at another example of using organizing and brainstorming software for activating prior knowledge. Mr. Corum, a high school history teacher, is beginning a unit on the U.S. Civil War and wants his students to have a clear understanding of their own beliefs and current thinking about its causes. He has several options for cueing and questioning students, including having them explore a Web Inquiry Project he found online at http://edweb.sdsu.edu/wip/. After allowing students 20 minutes to peruse the project or one of the other options, Mr. Corum moves into the next part of the lesson and opens Inspiration on a projected computer screen. The students watch as he types this question as the main idea: "What do you think caused the Civil War?" Then Mr. Corum selects the RapidFire tool on the toolbar, which lets him insert boxes or graphics with connectors in one move rather than individually so that he can keep up with the ideas that students are generating as they brainstorm aloud. As students enthusiastically offer their contributions, Mr. Corum records and organizes them for everyone to see. Figure 4.3 shows a snapshot of the class's brainstorming document. This map can be transformed into an outline with the click of a button. Later, students can skim the outline for ideas on the causes of the Civil War.

Figure 4.3
Brainstorming with Inspiration's RapidFire Tool

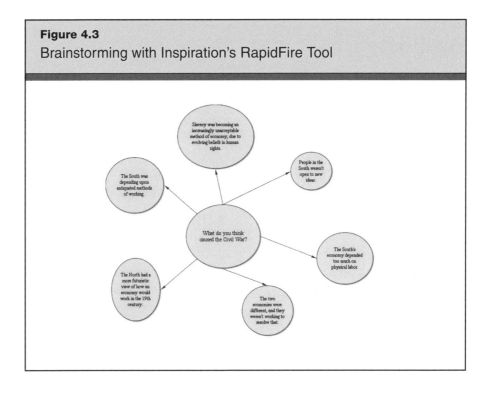

○ Multimedia

Using multimedia tools as advance organizers is an extension of expository, narrative, and graphic advance organizers. For many students, multimedia is very effective because it helps them both activate prior knowledge and develop a mental model to help them understand new information.

Generally speaking, expository advance organizers can be a very effective way to help students understand new content. Most teachers introduce new content by providing an overview of what's to come and asking students what they already know about the subject. A study on pupils' use of multimedia advance organizers and its effect on retention by Chien-Hsun Tseng (2004) found that students who were given a PowerPoint advance organizer to help articulate a lesson retained more information than those who did not receive this type of multimedia advance organizer.

Here's an example showing one teacher's creative application of this idea. To provide her students with a frame of reference as they begin reading John Steinbeck's *The Grapes of Wrath,* Ms. Simpson, a 10th grade language arts teacher, projects a PowerPoint slide show of images that capture the living conditions of displaced farm workers during the Great Depression. She reasons that the visuals will help her mostly affluent students, who have no real idea of hunger or hopelessness, gain a better sense of the hardships of that time period. While she knows that the pictures of the Dust Bowl period will make an impression on her students, she speculates that a movie will have an even greater impact. She visits the Yahoo! homepage (www.yahoo.com), clicks on Video at the top of the page, and types "Dust Bowl" in the Web Search window. The search returns 20 video clips related to the Dust Bowl, and Ms. Simpson previews and selects two to show to her students.

You can find video clips online from the following resources.

- United Streaming
www.unitedstreaming.com

Use this educational video collection to create an advance organizer at the onset of a learning activity.

- The Internet Archive
www.archive.org

Home to the "Way Back Machine" and Internet archives, this resource also has multiple video clips from the 20th century.

- Google Video
http://video.google.com

This search engine searches specifically for video clips using the keywords that you enter.

- A9
http://a9.com

From Amazon.com, this engine searches images, blogs, and movies in addition to books and Web sites.

- Creative Commons
http://creativecommons.org

Creative commons is a nonprofit organization that offers flexible copyright licenses for creative works. This engine searches for flexible copyright material—graphics, sounds, and publications—that are meant for public use. As students create videos as part of their learning, teachers can save the best of them on a flash drive, CD-ROM, or the school's server, and then use those videos as advance organizers with future classes.

This is just what one middle school teacher did when he required students to use the Internet and other resources to research an aspect of history that illustrates human rights and responsibilities. One group of girls created a movie about women's rights in China, titled *Grass Born To Be Stepped On*. Their final project is online at http://edcomunity.apple.com/ali/story.php?itemID=166. This year, the teacher is presenting a similar unit and begins by showing the girls' movie as a narrative advance organizer. In doing this, not only is the teacher illustrating how to use advance organizers, he is also highlighting nonlinguistic representation, providing feedback, and providing recognition. In Chapter 5's discussion of nonlinguistic representation, we'll revisit the topic of student-created videos and their affect on achievement.

Software with multimedia capabilities can also provide advance organizers. For example, Mrs. Lewers and her 6th graders are studying constellations, nebulas, and planets of the night sky. Over the next two weeks, she wants her students to find the Andromeda galaxy, which is the farthest celestial object visible to the naked eye. As preparation, she downloads a free, open-source program called Stellarium, which serves as a computer-based planetarium (www.stellarium.org). In class, she dims the lights, brings up Stellarium on a computer projector, and sets the current date and the school's location. She sets the local time as 8:00 p.m. so that her students can see what the sky above them will look like that evening.

Mrs. Lewers uses the arrow keys to navigate the software until the display shows the eastern sky and asks the students if they recognize any of the constellations that they see. Some correctly identify the "W" shape of Cassiopeia, so she hits a key that activates the constellation lines and titles in order for all to see (see Figure 4.4). She also asks her students to note a very small "smudge" of white near the star that creates the second "V" of Cassiopeia's "W." After selecting the Andromeda galaxy, she zooms in to give the class a magnified look.

With the software display serving as an advance organizer, students have a better idea of what to look for when they attempt to

Figure 4.4
Screen Shot of Stellarium with the Andromeda Galaxy Highlighted

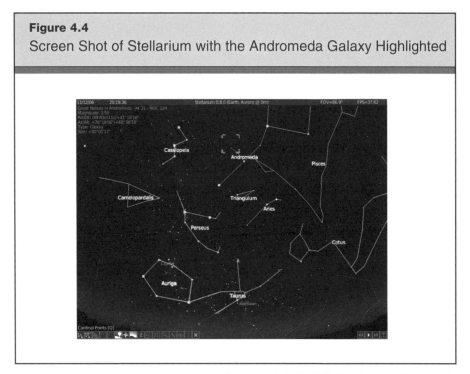

Image created with Stellarium (www.stellarium.org).

identify the constellation at home. Because the software is free, they also can ask their parents to download it for further practice.

Here's one more example showing how students can use multimedia as both an engaging advance organizer and a tool for practice. Ms. Wilson, a 1st grade teacher, wishes to provide her students with an advance organizer as they begin to study the clock and learn how to tell time. She goes to BrainPOP Jr. (www.brainpopjr.com), an online collection of short animated films for students in kindergarten through 3rd grade. Together, she and her students watch a movie about parts of the clock and follow with a short quiz. In Ms. Wilson's weekly letter home, she encourages parents to visit the site with their child to review the vocabulary and concepts covered in class that week.

5

NONLINGUISTIC
REPRESENTATION

Nonlinguistic representation enhances students' ability to use mental images to represent and elaborate on knowledge. To back up slightly, knowledge is stored in two forms: *linguistic* form (as language) and *nonlinguistic* form (as mental images and physical sensations). The more individuals use both types of representation, the better they are able to reflect on and recall knowledge. Teachers usually present new knowledge in linguistic form; that is, they either talk to students about new content or ask them to read about new content. When teachers branch out to help students use nonlinguistic representation as well, the effects on achievement are strong.

McREL's research on nonlinguistic representation supports the following generalizations:

GENERALIZATIONS

1. A variety of activities produce nonlinguistic representation. These are outlined in more detail in the classroom recommendations.
2. The purpose of nonlinguistic representation is to elaborate on knowledge.

Based on these findings, we have five recommendations for classroom practice:

RECOMMENDATIONS

1. Use graphic organizers to represent knowledge.
2. Have students create physical models of the knowledge.
3. Have students generate mental pictures of the knowledge they are learning.
4. Use pictures or pictographs to represent knowledge.
5. Have students engage in kinesthetic activities representing the knowledge.

Technology plays an obvious role in facilitating the creation of graphic organizers and helping to generate mental pictures and pictographs. According to Marzano's original meta-analysis (1998), using graphic representations had one of the highest impacts on student achievement, with an average effect size of 1.24. Another developing role of technology includes kinesthetic activities. New hardware and software that require the user to respond to and give information through physical sensations are currently in the beta test phase, which is the last stage of testing that a company engages in before introducing a new commercial product. In one such case, joysticks are being developed that react to a child's answers to a computer-based game. For example, if the child tries to place the letter *h* in the incorrect place in alphabetical order, the joystick will gently push back on his or her hand. This technology has been around for years in the training of pilots, surgeons, and astronauts; it is now making its way into the classroom. Nintendo has already launched a video game console called Wii that finally allows kinesthetic learners to fully apply their strengths to video games. The console controller fuses the familiarity of a remote control with the sophistication of motion-sensing technology. This Bluetooth input device allows for full-range movement. For example, in a tennis game, it serves as a racket you swing with your arm. In a driving game, it serves as your steering wheel. In addition to its pointing and motion-sensing abilities, the Wii remote also includes a speaker and rumble feature. It's only a matter of time before educators will be able to leverage this technology. Other examples of using kinesthetic activities with technology include Lego/Logo robotics and science probeware, such as temperature, light, and sound probes.

In this chapter, we look at six categories of technology that can help teachers provide and help students create mental pictures and pictographs: *word processing applications, spreadsheet applications, organizing and brainstorming software, data collection tools, multimedia applications,* and *Web resources.*

☉ Word Processing Applications

Word processing software allows students to augment their written text with visual elements such as clip art and photos. This strategy is especially helpful when working with emergent readers and English language learners, who benefit particularly from visual cues (Hill & Flynn, 2006). Adding pictures to notes also has been shown to improve students' understanding and retention of new content (Marzano, 1998).

Here's an illustration. Ms. Byers, a kindergarten teacher who is helping her students learn the sound of the letter *d,* brings up a word processing document on a computer projector, changes the type to 26-point Century Gothic (a font that young readers find very legible), and asks her students to think of words that start with the "d" sound. As students respond, she types a list of words, adding bold and underline formatting to the letter *d.* Ms. Byers then goes back and shows them how to insert clip art. She explains everything she does: "To add a drawing to each word, I'm going to place my cursor—that's the blinking line that you see—in front of each word. Then I'm going to go to "Insert." Can anyone tell me what the word *insert* would start with? Good, the letter *i.* Who sees the capital letter *I* up here in my menu? That's right; it's the fourth word in that row."

Ms. Byers continues cueing her students as she goes through the steps of adding clip art. (In this case, her clip art comes from www. clipart.com.) While the kindergarten students will not necessarily be able to insert clip art on their own for a while, they are seeing their teacher model the process. She lets various students choose the clip art that she pastes beside each word, and this way, she uses pictographs to help her students remember words that begin with the "d" sound. When they are finished, the list looks like Figure 5.1.

Figure 5.1
Graphics-Enhanced Notes: The Letter Sound "D"

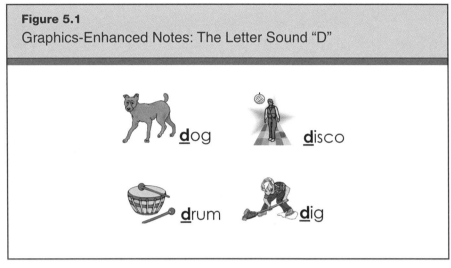

Clip art images © 2007 Jupiterimages Corporation.

Ms. Byers can now print the document and put copies in students' take-home folders, on the bulletin board, on each student's desk, on her classroom Web site, or any other place where the students will see the words and pictures and get a nonlinguistic reminder of the sound of the letter *d*.

This technique is easily used with upper elementary students to help them remember processes or new vocabulary words. A 4th grade teacher teaching about the life stages of butterflies might encourage her students to prepare for a quiz by creating a study guide featuring both pictures of the stages and a few descriptive words. The beginning stages of one student's study guide is shown in Figure 5.2.

○ Spreadsheet Software

One of spreadsheet software's primary purposes is to enable users to easily create graphs and charts from data entered. Although spreadsheet software is most often used in business settings, it can be a valuable classroom tool for creating nonlinguistic representation of data.

One effective way to use spreadsheet software in this manner comes from David Warlick (http://davidwarlick.com), an educational technology consultant and speaker. In an activity he demonstrates

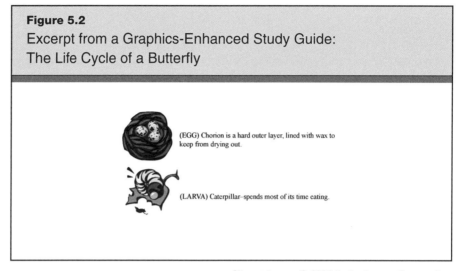

Figure 5.2
Excerpt from a Graphics-Enhanced Study Guide:
The Life Cycle of a Butterfly

(EGG) Chorion is a hard outer layer, lined with wax to keep from drying out.

(LARVA) Caterpillar-spends most of its time eating.

Clip art images © 2007 Jupiterimages Corporation.

for teachers, he begins by accessing data from the U.S. Geological Survey (http://neic.usgs.gov/neis/gis/qed.asc) that show seismic activity in the past 30 days: (see Figure 5.3). Most people look at this and can make little sense of these strings of numbers. Warlick then reformats the data and pastes them into Microsoft Excel, plotting the data on an XY scatter plot. If you'd like to follow along with his illustration, here are the steps to take:

1. With the Web page open, go to the Edit menu on your Web browser. Select All, and copy and paste the data into a Microsoft Word document.

2. In Word, make sure all the data are still selected (Edit > Select All if not) and under Table, click Convert > Text to Table. Make sure that Separate Text at option is selected to separate at Commas. Then click OK. You should now have a table with the following headings: Date, TimeUTC, Latitude, Longitude, Magnitude, and Depth.

3. Select the columns that show the Date, TimeUTC, Magnitude, and Depth. Right-click on these and Delete Columns. This removes the extraneous material for this particular activity, leaving only the latitude and longitude data.

4. The goal is to plot these coordinates on an *XY* plane, but latitude and longitude are in the opposite places to do this. In other words, if you leave column order as it is, you'll create a sideways map

Figure 5.3

Unformatted Seismic Data Downloaded
from the U.S. Geological Survey

```
Date,TimeUTC,Latitutde,Longitude,Magnitude,Depth
2006/03/27,09:06:08.5,-3.487,135.422,4.9, 42
2006/03/27,05:23:59.6-20.787,-69.428,5.3, 59
2006/03/27,02:50:27.5,32.516,131.789,5.3, 47
2006/03/27,01:10:33.0, 7.168,-34.261,5.3 ,10
2006/03/27,00:04:48.0,-15.587.-172.517,5.0, 35
2006/03/26,20:16:50.2,51.159,179.417,4.9, 48
2006/03/26,19:20:38.6,33.927,104,428,4.6, 3
2006/03/26,18:52:03.6,-6.699,127.356,4.5,412
2006/03/26,18:21:56.7,32.316,141.741,4.6, 10
2006/03/26,16:13:55.4m18,476,122.331,4.7, 7
2006/03/26,13:02:53.0,29.424,140.050,4.5, 35
2006/03/26,09:44:03.9,-28.846,-177.222,4.9, 59
2006/03/26,09:37:57.9,27.401, 55.895, 4.6,18
2006/03/26,05:49:53.1,-13.521,-76.992,4.7, 27
2006/03/26,05:14:53.1,-13.521,-76.992,4.7, 37
2006/03/26,02:24:37.4, 4.113,-78.619, 4.7, 37
2006/03/26,02:14:37.4,19.094,-64.821,4.4, 35
```

of the world. So select the Latitude column, Cut the column, and then select Paste Columns to paste it to the right of the Longitude column.

5. Select All again and Copy the entire table. (Both of these commands are found under the Edit menu.)

6. Now, it's time to get the spreadsheet software involved. Open a new Microsoft Excel document, and select Edit > Paste to paste the data into a spreadsheet.

7. Click on the Chart Wizard button on the Standard toolbar (it looks like a three-dimensional bar graph) and select the XY (Scatter). Type in a title for your chart, then click Finish.

The completed chart should look something like Figure 5.4.

A teacher who follows these steps will have changed what was initially a meaningless string of numbers into a nonlinguistic

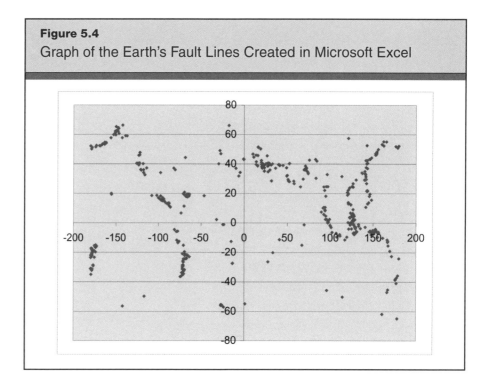

Figure 5.4
Graph of the Earth's Fault Lines Created in Microsoft Excel

representation of that data. Students will be able to see the plot points of the data and can begin to answer the following questions:

• Which line represents the equator?
• Which line represents the prime meridian?
• Where are the Aleutian Islands of Alaska?
• Where are the fault lines of California?
• How are the major plots showing at the 150-degree longitude mark related to natural disasters that have been on the news lately?

This approach is adaptable to a wide variety of lessons in which you want to help students make sense of data that initially seem confusing or overwhelming, such as longitudinal weather records or compounding interest over time.

The newest member of the Inspiration software family, Inspire-Data, allows students to enter data, then organize and sort it using nonlinguistic symbols and pictures in the Plot View. There are several options: Venn diagrams, stack graphs, and pie charts. Students can label the material in various ways, apply color schemes to indicate different data categories, and sort by label, color, and plot type.

○ Organizing and Brainstorming Software

Graphic representations serve as mnemonic devices that facilitate the classification, organization, storage, and recollection of information into and out of long-term memory. This is especially true for students with learning styles that favor visual forms of learning. Organizing and brainstorming software give teachers and students ways to create a variety of descriptive patterns to build conceptual understanding of everything from new vocabulary words to complex systems. In this way, teachers are addressing the classroom recommendation of using graphic organizers with their students.

Inspiration, Microsoft Visio, CmapTools, SmartTools (used with SmartBoards), and even the Microsoft Word Drawing toolbar can all be used to organize ideas and represent curricular concepts. You might start by using words and phrases in a pattern organizer and then add to them with visual, audible, and moving depictions. In this section, we demonstrate the value of the six common types of pattern organizers: conceptual/descriptive (combined for our example), generalization/principle, time-sequence, episode, and process/cause-effect.

Conceptual/Descriptive Pattern Organizers

Teachers can combine conceptual and descriptive pattern organizers in many ways and to many ends, including teaching facts and characteristics about a person, place, thing, event, or vocabulary word. This pattern type is more open-ended than the others and easy to create with students during classroom discussions. You can find some examples in Inspiration's Templates folder. See, for example, the Vocabulary Word template located under Language Arts and the Supporting Idea template located under Thinking Skills.

Figure 5.5 shows a descriptive pattern organizer for learning the vocabulary word *mnemonic*. It's a modification of the Vocabulary Word template found in Kidspiration's Reading and Writing Activities folder, created by a 5th grade teacher and his students to model how he wanted them to create their own descriptive pattern around vocabulary words. The students started the activity with words and then inserted images to deepen the learning and reinforce knowledge retention.

Figure 5.5

Conceptual/Descriptive Pattern Organizer Created
with Kidspiration's Vocabulary Word Template

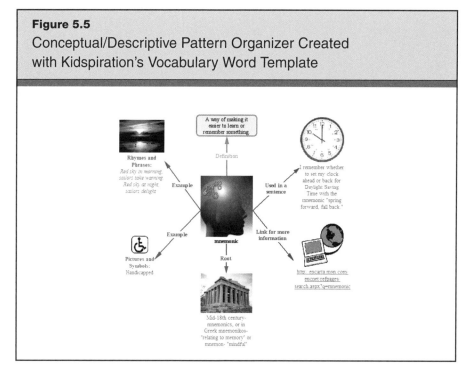

Clip art images © 2007 Jupiterimages Corporation.

Generalization/Principle Pattern Organizers

As their name suggests, generalization/principle pattern organizers work especially well in mathematics and science subjects. To illustrate, Ms. Scott's algebra students have been using quadratic equations for some time, and she expects them to understand the equations' applications. For a homework assignment, she provides an algebra principle and asks her students to make a pattern organizer with at least three different application examples. Because the students have previously worked with these mathematical principles and have already demonstrated their applications, no additional direct instruction is necessary. One of her students' organizers appears in Figure 5.6.

Time-Sequence Pattern Organizers

A time-sequence pattern organizer is terrific for teaching students historical progression. Say that Mrs. Campbell, a secondary social studies teacher, wants her students to understand the pace and events of the "Space Race" that started with Sputnik I in 1957 and

Figure 5.6

Generalization/Principle Pattern Organizer Created with the Microsoft Word Organization Chart

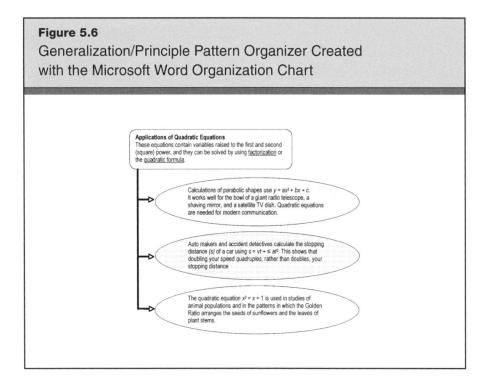

ended with the Apollo-Soyuz mission in 1975. She guides students in using Inspiration to create a Space Race Time Sequence like the one in Figure 5.7. She tells them to show both Soviet and U.S. missions and to incorporate symbols for the different types of space missions.

Alternatively, Mrs. Campbell could ask students to create a similar time-sequence pattern organizer using the Word Drawing tools. One technical hint she gives is to use the grid at Draw > Grid > Snap objects to grid and Draw > Grid > Display gridlines on screen. Mrs. Campbell also advises her students to use the clip art search located within Word at Insert > Picture > Clip Art so that they can be sure the images they select and use are not copyright-restricted.

Episode Pattern Organizers

Episode pattern organizers such as the one in Figure 5.8 are useful for depicting complex events where many different people, places, times, and processes all contribute to the overall concept. This type of graphic organizer also contains a time-sequence pattern within it. Our example is an extension of Mrs. Campbell's Space Race assignment. She chooses one of the best time-sequence organizers and uses it as part of a new episode pattern organizer as a way of discussing

Figure 5.7
Time-Sequence Pattern Organizer Created in Inspiration

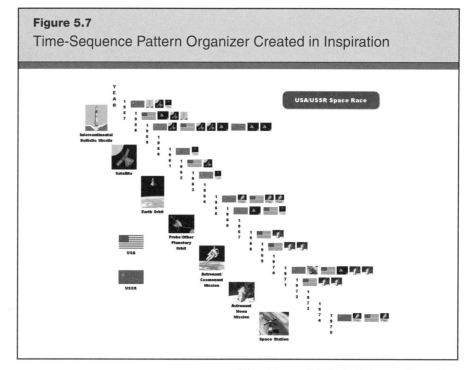

Clip art images © 2007 Jupiterimages Corporation.

the many factors involved with the Space Race. Mrs. Campbell creates the organizer seen in Figure 5.8 in Inspiration, then uses File > Transfer to Word Processor to place it in Microsoft Word. During class, she projects this organizer on screen and hyperlinks the time-sequence to the episode pattern organizer in Microsoft Word by using Insert > Hyperlink > Place in This Document > Space Race Time Sequence.

Process/Cause-Effect Pattern Organizers

The final example, in Figure 5.9, is a process/cause-effect pattern organizer. Here, a high school advisor opens a discussion of goals with freshmen participating in a group counseling session. The advisor uses the organizer to communicate the importance of sound planning practices and encourages the freshmen to make their own customized organizers. The visual helps students connect the decisions they make in high school to events later in life by allowing them to see possible cause-and-effect relationships at a glance. The organizer not only sparks discussion but guides it as well.

Figure 5.8
Episode Pattern Organizer Created in Inspiration

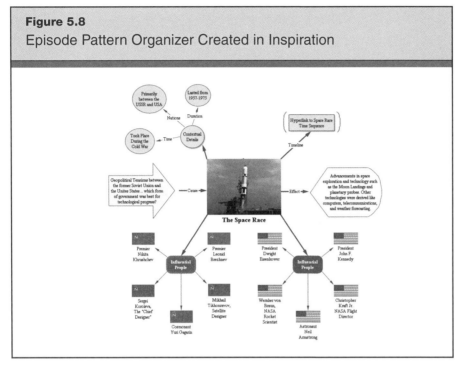

Launch photograph courtesy of the NASA Digital Image Collection.

Figure 5.9
Process/Cause-Effect Pattern Organizer
Created in Microsoft Word

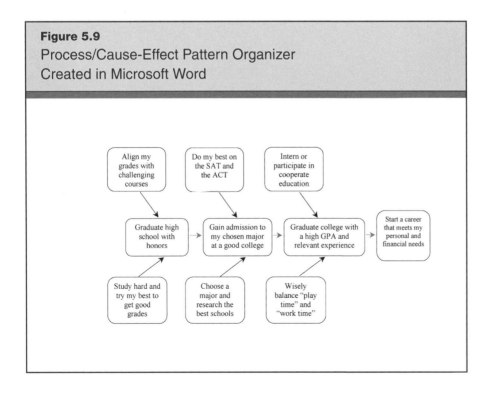

○ Data Collection Tools

Technology has come a long way in providing the tools that allow students to go beyond repetitive calculations, hand graphing, and sketching. Today's digital probes and digital microscopes feature photography and video functions that enable students to acquire information and images—some of which are types of nonlinguistic representation—for analysis, synthesis, and evaluation.

Obviously, probes and microscopes are useful tools in science class, but all subjects can use parts of these tools to enhance the curriculum. For instance, language arts and social studies classes might make use of digital scopes' photography and video functions in dramatic productions, anthropological investigations, and reenactments. Music classes might use sound probes to analyze music. Mathematics classes might use probe data to illustrate practical examples of graphing equations. Even so, let's use two science topics to illustrate the use of these two related technologies: first, how students can use digital probes to compare the temperatures and luminosity of incandescent and compact florescent light bulbs, and second, how students can use digital microscopes to examine both crystal patterns and *triops*, tiny prehistoric crustaceans that are among the oldest living species on the Earth.

Of course, to investigate the temperature and luminosity of light bulbs, students could also use the naked eye or standard thermometers and stopwatches, both of which were "high-tech" at one time. The next step would be to use graph paper and colored pencils to create graphs that incorporate observational data. Then, they might present this information by using a ruler to draw a large, approximate graph on a piece of poster board. These approaches are certainly sound; indeed, many of us learned by these very methods. Still, it is easy to see that modern technology has a lot to add in terms of efficiency, accuracy, analysis, and presentation. Likewise, students could observe crystals or triops with a magnifying glass, but a digital microscope greatly enhances this activity. Today's technology allows us to take still pictures, insert digital labels, record video clips, and use the resulting images in a presentation. The method is fast, easy, and produces professional looking results.

Digital Probes

For just about any science measurement that you can think of, you can collect data with a digital probe. Usually when you purchase probeware, it comes with software for data logging, analyzing, and graphing. Once students have learned the fundamentals of graphing, they can skip the boring, mistake-prone process of data entry and the time-consuming routine of creating hand-drawn graphs and get right to higher-level problem solving and thinking. Vendors such as Vernier, Pasco, HOBO, and Fourier specialize in different areas, such as wireless (Bluetooth) data transfer, long-term data logging, and all-in-one elementary multiprobes, but all of them allow the user to collect data and put them into a graphic form for further analysis, thereby following the classroom recommendation of using pictures or pictographs to represent information.

Here's an example of incorporating digital probes into a lesson. Mr. Enapay's 8th grade students are in the middle of a science inquiry investigation. Mr. Enapay helps his students use Vernier probes to compare different types of light bulbs. (Vernier has two versions of their data-logging software: an elementary version called Logger Lite and a version for older students called Logger *Pro.*) Last year, his students used thermometers and graphed the data by hand. It was an inaccurate and slow process. He is hoping things will go more smoothly this year with the school's new probes.

Mr. Enapay explains to his students that compact fluorescent and incandescent light bulbs produce light from electricity in different ways. They each emit a specific amount of light, called *luminosity,* which is measured in lumens/m^2 or *lux*. They each last for an approximate amount of time, measured in hours of use. The heat that both bulbs generate is measured in degrees Celsius per second.

Mr. Enapay's students use the probes to collect luminosity and heat data simultaneously, The accompanying Logger *Pro* software graphs these data instantly (see Figure 5.10). When students add these data to other data, such as price and the manufacturer's rated power, they get a good idea of how the bulbs compare and, thus, which one is the better buy. With digital probes, they can also measure luminosity and heat over time. Students save their graphs for later use in a presentation.

Mr. Enapay observes that by using probes, his students spend much less time calculating and representing data, which is on the lower level of Bloom's taxonomy, and more time working at the higher levels: analyzing and evaluating the graphic patterns to decide the short- and long-term pros and cons of using each type of light bulb.

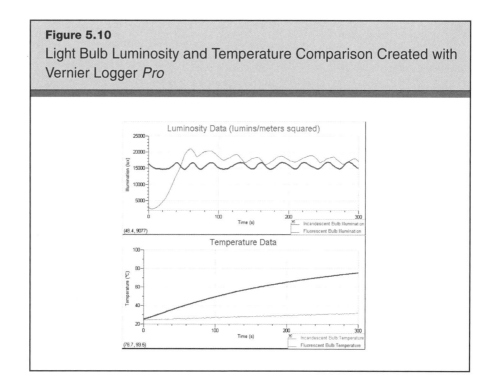

Figure 5.10

Light Bulb Luminosity and Temperature Comparison Created with Vernier Logger *Pro*

In Vernier's elementary-friendly software application, Logger Lite, the interface has large, easy-to-read buttons, which help young students to see the data. Ms. Cobb, a kindergarten teacher, uses a digital probe and Logger Lite to help her students understand the concept of insulation. She begins by asking them why they think that their mittens and gloves keep their hands warm in the winter. Some students hypothesize that the mittens themselves are warm. To test this theory—and to demonstrate the concept of insulation—Ms. Cobb takes a reading of the classroom's temperature by setting the probe on her desk. While the numerical degrees might not be meaningful, the students are able to see the line that represents the temperature, and they will be able to observe the line falling or rising as the temperature changes. Ms. Cobb then places the probe inside an empty mitten. The students observe that nothing changes. However, when a volunteer comes up and places his hand in the mitten with the probe still in place, the students see that the temperature begins to rise. They now have a better understanding that it is the hand inside a mitten that actually creates heat, and the mitten contains that heat. By using the software, Ms. Cobb presents her kindergarteners with a vivid, nonlinguistic picture of the data that they can understand without having to decipher numbers and degrees.

Digital Microscopes

Most microscope manufacturers make a microscope that can export images to a computer. However, the most versatile digital microscopes are those that can be used both in a traditional, mounted configuration and as a handheld field scope. Unlike traditional microscopes, digital scopes have the built-in capacity to take pictures, movies, and time-lapse images. Some types also can project onscreen images, such as pages in a book or magazine articles, when they're plugged into a computer's USB port for data transfer and power. Scope vendors and manufacturers such as ProScope, Konus, Ken-A-Vision, Prime Entertainment, and Scalar sell various models of handheld and mountable digital USB scopes. These usually come with their own proprietary software, which is compatible with many image-viewing programs standard to the most common computer operating systems.

Teachers can have students use digital microscopes both during their investigations and afterward to create diagrams and graphics for students' analyses and presentations. Figure 5.11 shows pictures of microscopic topaz crystals taken with a ProScope. With the unaided eye, it's impossible to tell their crystal shape, and they don't make good specimens for a typical microscope because they have an uneven surface and would not fit on a microscope slide. However, with a digital scope, you can take magnified pictures of their uneven surface. This allows you to find crystals that exhibit a perfect natural shape. While uneven formation conditions and impurities cause many of the crystals to deform, you can find a few that form just right. Can you find the hexagonal crystals in these pictures?

Figure 5.11
Pictures of Topaz Crystals Taken with a
ProScope Digital Microscope

Digital scopes also provide a way to produce video clips of live microscopic specimens. Figure 5.12 shows another image captured with a ProScope: the first frame in a video clip documenting a triop swimming in a Petri dish. Triops, tiny creatures that date back to the Triassic Period, live in intermittent pond environments. They hatch, breed, and die within 90 days, and their eggs can last for decades waiting for a strong rain to fill the pond.

Figure 5.12
Video Image of a Triop Taken
with a ProScope Digital Microscope

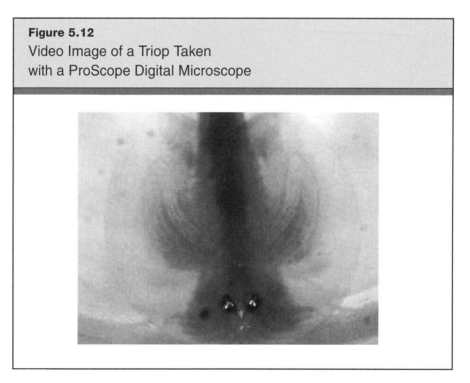

Finally, many digital scopes allow students to create time-lapse movies. Figure 5.13 shows a frame from a time-lapse movie documenting plant growth, created by Mr. Fuglestad's science students at Stillwater Junior High School in Stillwater, Minnesota. Projects that involve monitoring changes over time and recording data reinforce the science skills of observation. And with digital scopes, students can capture phenomena that might otherwise go unnoticed.

Figure 5.13

Frame of a Time-Lapse Movie on Plant Growth

Special thanks to Stillwater Junior High and science teacher Pete Fuglestad.

⟳ Multimedia

One of the most effective forms of nonlinguistic representation is multimedia. Since teachers first started showing reel-to-reel films in their classrooms, countless educators have observed that movies and videos help engage students in content. Today, we can take that engagement much further by shifting multimedia learning from something that's teacher-directed to something that's teacher-facilitated. Research indicates that multimedia has the most effect on student learning when the student is the creator (Siegle & Foster, 2000). Although PowerPoint presentations and movies are great teaching aids and do lead to higher levels of student engagement, the most engaging learning comes from having the student create the presentation or movie themselves as a part of the learning process. Many believe that the movie-editing tools that have become ubiquitous in schools are leading to a new "digital literacy," in which students need to know the language of camera angle, colors, soundtrack, and fonts in much the same way that they need to know the grammar of written and spoken language. George Lucas (2005) likens this evolving literacy to the onset of reading and writing in the general population that followed the invention of the printing press.

It is essential that students understand the significance of copyright and fair use, and this is especially imperative when they engage in multimedia projects. Students should know, for example, that according to Section 4.2.3 of Consortium of College and University Media Centers' *Fair Use Guidelines for Educational Multimedia* (1996), they should not sample more than 10 percent or 30 seconds of the song. Students should be aware of these guidelines, but also should be introduced to open-access sources that have more relaxed laws regarding student use. For instance, they can go to www.freeplaymusic.com and download entire songs free of charge for an education-related movie. Web sites such as http://creativecommons.org help students and teachers to locate audio, video, images, text, and educational resources for their projects.

Multimedia is a combination of single mediums, such as video, audio, and interactivity. Generally, we can think of multimedia in the classroom as projects that include at least two of the following: audio, video, graphics, animations, and text. Thus, multimedia projects might include presentations, animations, and movies created in the software applications such as Inspiration, PowerPoint, iMovie, and Movie Maker. These types of projects help students create a mental image of the concepts and themes they are trying to learn. Think back to a memorable project you did in school. Did it involve some sort of imagery or visual aids? As we have stated before, knowledge connected with nonlinguistic representation is remembered more deeply than with linguistic forms alone.

Presentations

The advancement of presentation technology is one of the most powerful innovations in educational technology. With some creativity, a computer, a projector, and presentation software, students can create presentations that rival those of professionals. Although PowerPoint is not the only software used for classroom presentations, it is by far the most dominant. Browse these Web sites to get some ideas about student and teacher presentations:

- Jefferson County Schools—PowerPoint Collection
http://jc-schools.net/ppt.html

This is a large collection of K–12 student and teacher PowerPoint presentations in all subjects.

- Project-Based Learning with Multimedia
http://office.microsoft.com/en-us/help/HA011411961033.aspx

Here, you'll find free education presentation resources from Microsoft.

- Educational PowerPoint Templates
www.paducah.k12.ky.us/curriculum/PPoint/

This is a collection of presentation templates for elementary topics. These templates are good for students and teachers just learning to create multimedia presentations.

- PowerPoint in the Classroom
www.actden.com/pp

This is a fun, colorful Web site with two cartoon characters to guide you (or your students) through the basics of PowerPoint.

- Keynote User Tips
www.keynoteuser.com/tips/index.html

This site has themes, tips, links, troubleshooting, and other cool stuff for Apple's Keynote presentation software.

- Keynote Theme Park
www.keynotethemepark.com/index.html

This is an ideal Web site for finding free theme downloads, recommended links, news, and tips.

- HyperStudio Tutorial
www.k12.hi.us/~tethree/01-02/tutorials/hs/home1.html

HyperStudio is an alternative multimedia-authoring software application. This site provides "how to's" and examples for HyperStudio.

As students begin a multimedia project, too often their first step is to launch the software and begin to haphazardly, if enthusiastically, create something. Presentations, and movies even more so, require significant planning and organization. Otherwise, students can get carried away in the fun aspects of production and not pay enough attention to the content, resulting in a "PowerPointless" presentation. Remember, content is what it's all about. Good presentations should follow the same steps as moviemaking, which we will discuss later in this section.

Students should begin a PowerPoint project just as they would any other research project and should only move into the presentation software *after* they have completed their background research, planning, and draft writing. (An exception to this guideline is when the objective of the lesson is to learn a particular PowerPoint skill.) In general, students should try and answer the tried and true questions of *who, what, where, when, why,* and *how.* As they delve deeper into the whys and hows of a project, they practice problem solving and analysis, and use other higher-level thinking skills. Of course, the teacher's responsibility is to refine these questions based on the new content, students' learning goals, and the type of project being undertaken.

For teachers preparing students to engage in a multimedia project, developing the scoring rubric is a critical step. When you are adapting or creating a multimedia project rubric, ask yourself several questions: How long do you really want the students' presentations to be? How much computer space is available? Who is the audience? Which software is compatible? Here are some specific items to consider in a project rubric:

1. Content accuracy
2. Length of presentation (number of slides)
3. Slide layout (e.g., amount of text and number of graphics, titles, sounds, animations)
4. Background graphics appropriate for audience and theme

5. Software requirements (e.g., Quicktime, Java, Flash, Windows Media Player)

6. File size (compressing pictures will help a lot with this)

7. Storage and delivery requirements

8. Color schemes

When planning, it is preferable to build-in enough time for every student to present his or her project for the entire class. With so much to teach, time is always a concern, and we realize that you may not be able to allow all of your students to present in each unit. A good compromise is to randomly select a small number of presenters—perhaps three to five students per assignment. Of course, students who do not present must still turn in a digital or printed copy of their project. Alternately, you could ask all students to present a short-ened version of their presentation. This way, all students practice creating projects and learn more about the communication skills required to present.

Figure 5.14 shows an example of a student-created slide for a pre-sentation on Martin Luther King Jr.'s influence on American society.

Most of the slides in this presentation do not contain as many types of multimedia as this one, nor should they. However, this slide is a good example of how sound, video, text, and imagery can be com-bined in an effective presentation. Notice how the slide has a title, template, and logo. It also has hyperlinked sound and video. The sound and video files are saved in the same folder as the PowerPoint file, with hyperlinks attached to the words "Watch the Speech" and "Listen to the Speech." Also, notice how the text has been placed over areas of the images that are not critical but have been shadowed to maintain the images' original look and allow for enough contrast to read the text. This shadowing is done by putting the text in a textbox, changing the text color to contrast with the background, highlighting the textbox, and choosing Format > Text Box > Colors and Lines > (choose a color) > Transparency = 50% > OK.

Animations

As children, many of us made animations. We used a tablet of paper and drew stick figures, making slight changes in the stick figures' positions on each page. Then we quickly flipped through the pages

Figure 5.14
Slide in a PowerPoint Multimedia Presentation

License for photos of Martin Luther King Jr. granted by Intellectual Properties Management, Atlanta, Georgia, as exclusive licensor of the King Estate. Photo of the March on Washington reproduced with permission of AP/Wide World Photos.

and watched our rudimentary animation. Whether it is our stick figure flipbooks or an animated movie like Pixar's *The Incredibles,* all animations share basic beginnings. Here are three quality online resources that will help you and your students learn more about animation:

• Webmonkey for Kids
http://webmonkey.com/webmonkey/kids

This site has in-depth tutorials in GIF animation, dHTML, and Flash.

• Animation Factory
www.animationfactory.com/help/tutorial_gif.html

This site has tutorials from Animation Factory by Jupiterimages and a collection of royalty-free animated clip art on the Internet. It features more than 400,000 animations, video backgrounds, PowerPoint templates, backdrops, and Web graphics.

- Animation Inspirations
www.apple.com/uk/education/animation

This is a stop-motion animation tutorial from Apple Education.

Here is one of the simplest way to teach students to animate. Explain to your class that they will animate their ideas by creating a series of progressing diagrams, and ask them to begin by drawing a *template frame* as the starting point for the scene they want to animate. (You may have noticed that the background scenery in old cartoons doesn't change much. This is because those cartoons were made using a template frame.) This frame can be drawn in any software program that will generate a picture, such as Word, PowerPoint, or Photoshop. Next, explain to students that they can add, subtract, or modify images within the template frame using copy, paste, and rotate commands as well as other drawing tools, such as those found in the Drawing toolbar in Word. Have students save the frame they create by number and scene (unless there is only one scene). Then ask students to save their modified frame as the next frame in the series and continue animating until all of the frames are complete. Finally, they should save the edited version in a movie format, using moviemaking software such as iMovie or Windows Movie Maker. If your class does not have access to this specialized software, they could create simple animated movies using just the animation and looping features in PowerPoint.

In Figure 5.15, you can see some student-created frames for an animation demonstrating a chemical reaction in which concentrated sulfuric acid dehydrates sucrose to produce carbon and water. Notice the slides' sequential titling and how the student drew the beaker and reaction chamber once and then rotated and moved these elements in subsequent slides. Each slide is one frame of the animation; when connected together in a series, they create the illusion of movement.

ToonBoom Animation Inc. creates software that aids in learning animation processes. Other approaches to animation include using still images, time-lapse photography, and manipulated objects, such as paper cut-outs, puppets, or clay figures (claymation). Not surprisingly, the creative and kinesthetic aspects of animation of manipulated objects can be particularly engaging for young students.

Figure 5.15
Frames for an Animation

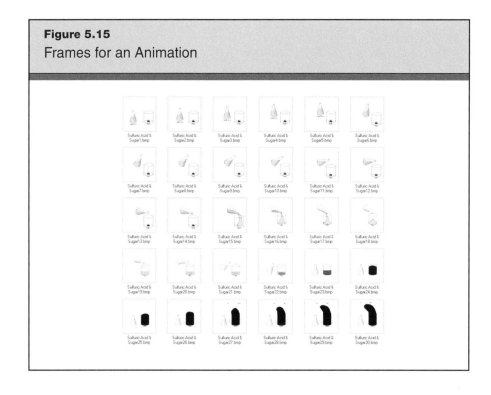

Consider the example of a 1st grade teacher who will conclude a unit on the Amazon Rainforest by assessing students' understanding of the rainforest's animals and their habitat. She announces that the class will be creating a claymation movie, and that each student will be using clay to create two animals that live in the Amazon Rainforest. The teacher goes on to help the students to look up each animal's eating habits, determine which level of the rainforest it lives in (e.g., in the canopy, at ground level), and find three interesting facts about it. Then, the class turns this information into a movie script. When filming begins, each student places his or her animals on the correct backdrop and poses them in various positions as the teacher takes a series of pictures. The students are also involved in recording the script narration, reinforcing the skills of reading aloud fluently. When all of the pictures have been taken and the narration has been recorded, the teacher demonstrates how the images can be combined into an animated movie with sound overlaid. Figure 5.16 shows Audra's anteater, a frame from the 1st graders' finished claymation movie.

Figure 5.16
Frame from a Claymation Movie

Special thanks to Steve Tromly.

Movies and Video

We approach using movies and video as a form of nonlinguistic representation from two perspectives: using them *for* instruction and using them *as* instruction. The first case is the example of using a streaming video or DVD to engage learners and build background knowledge. We have discussed this use of movies in earlier sections of this book (see Chapter 4's discussion of multimedia, page 88). The following example of how Mrs. Robinson, a middle school science teacher, integrates movies into her instruction on writing in the content area also demonstrates this function, but in a slightly different way.

First, Mrs. Robinson modifies a story-writing rubric using RubiStar. She then attaches the completed rubric to a list of astronomy vocabulary terms that students have been learning. She gives students the assignment to write a story using at least 10 of the following astronomy terms in correct context:

escape velocity	gravity	ionosphere
magnetosphere	meteoroid	pressure
radiation	reaction engine	rotation
satellite	thrust	weight
geosynchronous orbit		

After Mrs. Robinson gives students the rubric and list of vocabulary words, she asks them to read the terms carefully, think about what each one means, and think about how they could incorporate the terms into their stories according to the standards set by the rubric. The next thing she does surprises students and heightens their interest in the assignment. Mrs. Robinson adds a third element to the assignment: a nonlinguistic representation in the form of a music video. She tells the students to get comfortable, turns down the lights, and projects the music video of the 1983 song "Major Tom (Coming Home)" by Peter Schilling (inspired by David Bowie's 1969 hit "Space Oddity") from a free downloaded version she found on the Internet at www.vh1.com/artists/az/schilling_peter/artist.jhtml. Sometimes she shows a student-made music video of Bowie's original song, found at http://video.google.com (search: *Daydreaming to David Bowie*). By the time the brief video is over, Mrs. Robinson's students have generated mental pictures that give the vocabulary context. Now they have plenty of creative ideas and are well prepared to use the vocabulary terms in their stories.

The second way movies are used in the classroom involves students actually creating the movies themselves to demonstrate their knowledge and skills. Generally, students enjoy the challenge, creativity, and collaboration that go into creating movies, and research shows that students have a higher level of understanding and retention when they learn with media and technology (Reeves, 1998; Siegle & Foster, 2000). You also can use the movies they create over and over again as examples for other students. The section on Web resources, beginning on page 62, includes some great examples of student-created movies. But first, let's take a look at the steps students should follow to create their own movies. Please note that these steps are additional to other assignment requirements, such as those set in a project rubric.

Step 1: Writing the script. The script consists of the exact words that the student actors will read or speak. To be sure of the timing, the actors should read the script aloud and time it. Remind them to allow time for pauses or transitions between ideas.

Step 2: Storyboarding. The purpose of the storyboard is to give students an idea of the images, settings, and props they will need for the movie. Tell them that as they read their scripts, they might decide that "a picture is worth a thousand words." Instead of describing something dramatic, why not show it?

At this point, students should transfer the script to the lines on the storyboard, breaking it into sections dictated by the images that should accompany the lines. In the box for each section, students might describe or draw a picture that reminds them of the image they want at that point in the movie. If they are using still images, they should notate where those images are stored on the computer, or note that they need to take the picture. If they use Web sites, they should write the site's URL. Figure 5.17 shows two examples from a student-movie storyboard. Note that the students have titled the scene, numbered each shot, and included the relevant lines from the script, along with tips for filming and editing.

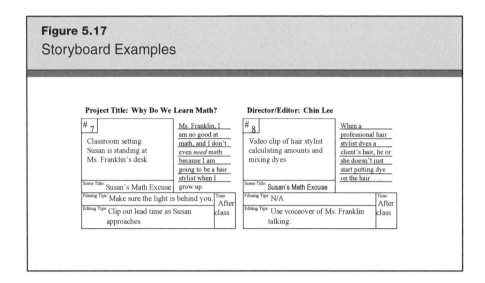

Figure 5.17
Storyboard Examples

Step 3: Shooting the video. In the classroom, this step involves resource allocation. Most classrooms have a limited number of still and video cameras available. Before issuing a camera to students, review their scripts and storyboards for completion and verify that they have conducted at least one full practice speaking their lines with props. Also, if students plan to shoot still pictures, they should have all needed materials. If they plan to have a voiceover effect in their movies, they should record the spoken words on camera beforehand. It is easier to import a video clip and separate the audio during the editing process.

Here are some tips on recording video to pass along to students:

• Begin recording three to five seconds before the actor starts talking. You might need this space during the editing process.

• Use a tripod to keep the camera steady.

• Use a digital microphone rather than the one on the camera. This will improve the sound quality. A clip-on microphone works well.

• It is not necessary to shoot the video sequentially. If you are using different scenes, you can shoot all the video in one scene before moving to the next, even if the scenes you shoot aren't in the same order as the movie.

• *Remember:* Every time the video camera stops recording, the video software makes a new video clip.

Step 4: Importing the video and images. Importing the video into iMovie (Macintosh) or Movie Maker (Windows) is as simple as connecting the digital video camera to the computer's Firewire or USB port and launching either iMovie or Movie Maker. If your students are using a different Windows version, they will need to have a video editing software program like Adobe Premiere. Follow your software's steps for importing video.

Step 5: Video editing. Now is the time to refer back to the storyboard. Students should have a collection of video clips, still images, and audio clips on a computer. They might also want to use the computer's microphone to "lay down" an audio track that will play under a series of still or video images. Students should collaborate in the editing process. Feedback from others is particularly valuable because, in students' minds, their story is well told, but as others see the video with fresh eyes, it's more likely they will be able to point out parts that are confusing or scenes that seem to be missing. Once the clips are in the correct order, students might need to edit individual clips, removing unwanted sections. They should edit all clips before adding the transitions between them.

Once the movie is rough-edited, students can add a title at the beginning and credits at the end. Remind them in the assignment guidelines to cite sources in the credits. This is great opportunity to teach or review proper citation formats. One good reference site is hosted by Duke University Libraries at www.lib.duke.edu/libguide/

cite/works_cited.htm. It has examples of various kinds of citations in APA, MLA, Chicago, Turabian, and CSE formats. As previously mentioned, it is important to both model and monitor copyright compliance.

Step 6: Adding music. Now students will add appropriate music. While students will want to use their own CDs or music they have obtained online, it is important to model ethical behavior. Because the movies they are creating are for educational purposes, they may incorporate copyrighted music, provided that they purchased this music legally and limit the selected clips to no more that 30 seconds or 10 percent of the song's full length, whichever is less. You might want to direct students to use the sound clips in the moviemaking software or go to www.freeplaymusic.com and find the style and length of music that meets the needs of their movie. All the music at Freeplaymusic is copyright-free, but students should still cite the source in the credits.

Step 7: Saving and sharing the movie. Now students should make sure they have saved their movie in its final form. This usually involves condensing all the separate pieces into one movie file. At this point, they are ready to share the movie with the class, the school, the community, and maybe even the wider world via the Internet, as mentioned in Chapter 3's discussion of providing recognition.

Web Resources

Let's look again at the use of multimedia *for* instruction rather than *as* instruction. McREL's meta-analysis, *A Theory-Based Meta-Analysis of Research on Instruction* (Marzano, 1998) discusses specific teaching strategies and the effect sizes on student achievement. Marzano found that "the use of computer simulation as the vehicle with which students manipulate artifacts produced the highest effect size of 1.45 (n = 1), indicating a percentile gain of 43 points" (p. 91).

There are great computer simulations available on the Web, some for free and others by subscription. One outstanding example of a free simulation resource is the National Library of Virtual Manipulatives (http://nlvm.usu.edu/en/nav/vlibrary.html). This site provides scores of interactive Java applications. Students select from a matrix organized by content area (numbers and operations, algebra, geometry, measurement, and data analysis and probability) and by grade level (preK–2, 3–5, 6–8, and 9–12.) Figure 5.18 shows an example of an algebra simulation for high school students.

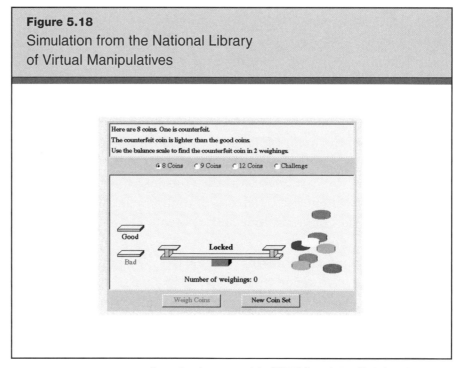

Figure 5.18
Simulation from the National Library
of Virtual Manipulatives

Here are 8 coins. One is counterfeit.
The counterfeit coin is lighter than the good coins.
Use the balance scale to find the counterfeit coin in 2 weighings.

⦿ 8 Coins   ◯ 9 Coins   ◯ 12 Coins   ◯ Challenge

Good

Bad

Locked

Number of weighings: 0

Weigh Coins   New Coin Set

Reproduced courtesy of the MATTI Association, Utah State University.

Each simulation at this site also includes a link to the national standards it addresses, a teacher/parent guide, and instructions for the student.

Elementary students will love the multimedia simulations found on iKnowthat.com (www.iknowthat.com). This site has interactive multimedia applications for preK–6 language arts, mathematics, science, social studies, the arts, and problem solving. If a subscription-based site is an option, ExploreLearning (www.explorelearning.com) is a great source for simulations. It offers a catalog of modular, interactive simulations, called gizmos, in mathematics and science for teachers and students in grades 6–12. One example is the "mouse genetics" gizmo in Figure 5.19. In this simulation, students breed "pure" mice with known genotypes that exhibit specific fur and eye colors, and thus learn how traits are passed on via dominant and recessive genes. They can store mice in virtual cages for future breeding and get statistics on fur and eye color every time a pair of mice breeds. They can use Punnett squares to predict results. While it's true that students can read about genotypes in a textbook, using a simulation like this one allows them to see the effects of genetics over 100 generations in less than two minutes.

Figure 5.19
ExploreLearning's Mouse Genetics Gizmo

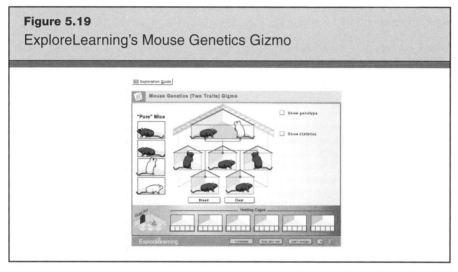

Reproduced courtesy of ExploreLearning.

Here are some other quality Web resources that can support nonlinguistic representation:

- Knowitall.org
www.knowitall.org

Knowitall.org is South Carolina ETV's educational Web portal, a collection of fun, interactive Web sites for K–12 students. The site is searchable by both subject and grade level and has support resources for teachers and parents.

- Surviving Everest
http://channel.nationalgeographic.com/channel/highspeed/everest

This interactive site by National Geographic allows students to explore the conditions that climbers must endure while scaling Mount Everest. Streaming video from each stage in the climb gives students eyewitness views of the climb.

- Interactive Mathematics Activities
www.cut-the-knot.org/Curriculum/index.shtml

Java-based mathematics games are categorized by discipline. This site is very appropriate for high school and even college students. In addition to algebra and geometry, there are games for logic, calculus, probability, and more.

- Clay Animation in PowerPoint
www.pendergast.k12.az.us/edservices/as/wow/claytutorial.pdf

Combining claymation and PowerPoint is an engaging and powerful way for students to create meaningful electronic presentations. This online multimedia presentation provides a step-by-step tutorial for creating stop-motion clay animations and bringing them to life in PowerPoint.

- DigiTales: The Art of Telling Digital Stories
www.digitales.us

Bernajean Porter's DigiTales Web site provides tools and examples to help teachers and students begin the process of digital storytelling. A section on evaluating student projects includes rubrics and scoring guides.

- Our TimeLines
www.ourtimelines.com

This free Web resource allows students to create a timeline of a person within the context of events that happened during his or her lifetime. Categories of events include historical events, technological advances, and disasters.

- iCan Film Festival
www.sfett.com

The San Fernando Education Technology Team's iCan Film Festival page is possibly the best online collection of student-created movies, produced under the guidance of Marco Torres, an Apple Distinguished Educator and 2005 California Teacher of the Year.

6

SUMMARIZING AND NOTE TAKING

The instructional strategy *summarizing and note taking* focuses on enhancing students' ability to synthesize information and distill it into a concise new form. Here, teachers work on helping students separate important information from extraneous information and state the information in their own words.

McREL's research on summarizing supports the following generalizations:

GENERALIZATIONS

1. To effectively summarize, students must delete some information, substitute some information, and keep some information.
2. To effectively delete, substitute, and keep information, students must analyze the information at a fairly deep level.
3. Being aware of the explicit structure of information is an aid to summarizing information.

Based on these findings, we have three recommendations for classroom practice:

RECOMMENDATIONS

1. Teach students the rule-based summarizing strategy.
2. Use summary frames.
3. Teach students the reciprocal teaching strategy.

Note taking is similar to summarizing in that it enhances students' ability to organize information in a way that captures the main ideas and supporting details, helping students to process information. Although note taking is one of the most useful study skills a student can cultivate, teachers rarely teach it explicitly as a skill in itself.

McREL's research on note taking supports the following generalizations:

GENERALIZATIONS

1. Verbatim note taking is perhaps the least effective way to take notes.
2. Notes should be considered a work in progress.
3. Notes should be used as study guides for tests.
4. The more notes that are taken, the better.

Based on these findings, we have three recommendations for classroom practice:

RECOMMENDATIONS

1. Give students teacher-prepared notes.
2. Teach students a variety of note-taking formats.
3. Use combination notes.

Technology, in the form of typewriters and word processors, has been playing a role in note taking for many years. Now, however, the sophistication of the software available can turn it into true learning experiences. Technology can scaffold, or provide support, while students are learning the summarizing process. It can also provide collaborative summarizing experiences that facilitate *reciprocal teaching*, a very structured format for helping students to teach each other developed by Palincsar and Brown (1984, 1985). In this section, we show you how *word processing applications, organizing and brainstorming software, multimedia, Web resources,* and *communication software* help to scaffold and organize the summarizing and note-taking processes.

○ Word Processing Applications

A word processor is a computer application used to produce printable material. These run the gamut from the robust Microsoft Word to the free Google Docs and Spreadsheets program. All provide teachers a way to strengthen summarizing and note taking.

Summarizing

One classroom recommendation for teaching students to summarize in the classroom is to use rule-based summarizing. This strategy provides students with a process to apply as they summarize and gives them a structure to guide them when attempting what can otherwise be a confusing task. Figure 6.1 shows the steps for rule-based summarizing that, with slight modifications, apply to both younger and older students.

You can use the Track Changes feature in Microsoft Word to both demonstrate rule-based summarizing and have students practice the

---

Figure 6.1
Rule-Based Summarizing

Steps for Younger Students
1. Take out the material that is not important to understanding.
2. Take out words that repeat information.
3. Replace a list of things with a word that describes the things in the list (e.g., use the word *trees* for *elm, oak,* and *maple*).
4. Find a topic sentence. If you can't find a topic sentence, write one.

Steps for Older Students
1. Delete trivial material that is unnecessary to understanding.
2. Delete redundant material.
3. Substitute superordinate terms for more specific terms (e.g., use *fish* for *trout, salmon,* and *halibut*).
4. Select a topic sentence or invent one if it is missing.

process. First, open Word and go to Tools > Track Changes to activate the feature. To be sure the Track Changes options are set correctly, go to Tools > Options. Now click on the Track Changes tab. Be sure to select Strikethough next to the word Deletions. Your finished Options window should look like the illustration in Figure 6.2. When done, click OK and close the options window.

Figure 6.2
Track Changes Option Screen in Microsoft Word

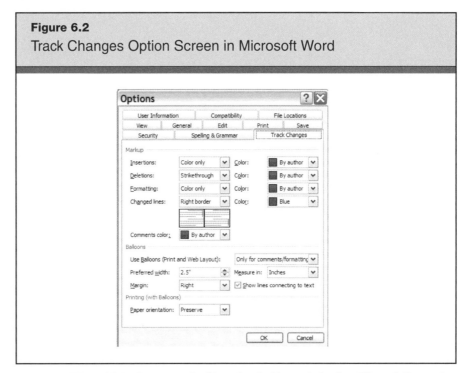

Microsoft® product screen shot(s) reprinted with permission from Microsoft Corporation.

Here's how Ms. Sanborn, a 7th grade science teacher, uses the Track Changes feature to show her students how to summarize a selection from their textbook. She begins by selecting a passage from her textbook and typing it into a blank Word document. After saving the document, she activates Track Changes as we've explained and begins applying the summarizing rules. As Ms. Sanborn finds a sentence that is redundant, she highlights it and presses the delete key. As you see in Figure 6.3, that section appears crossed out. You can also see where she simplifies the terms "continents and tectonic plates" to "land surfaces."

Figure 6.3

Microsoft Word Document Showing Tracked Changes

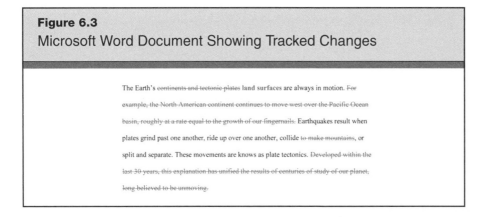

The Earth's ~~continents and tectonic plates~~ land surfaces are always in motion. ~~For example, the North American continent continues to move west over the Pacific Ocean basin, roughly at a rate equal to the growth of our fingernails.~~ Earthquakes result when plates grind past one another, ride up over one another, collide ~~to make mountains~~, or split and separate. These movements are knows as plate tectonics. ~~Developed within the last 30 years, this explanation has unified the results of centuries of study of our planet, long believed to be unmoving.~~

By modeling the process for her students using the word processor, Ms. Sanborn is able to show them how to summarize the text in a way that makes it easier for them to understand the content.

Another useful feature in Word that many teachers don't know about is the AutoSummarize tool. It does exactly what the name suggests: takes a selection of text and provides a summary. Let's use the same excerpt from Figure 6.3 to show how AutoSummarize works. First, we take the excerpt and paste it into a new Word document. Now we go to Tools > Auto Summarize. The resulting screen gives us a choice of four different summary options: (1) Highlight the key points; (2) insert an executive summary at the top of the document; (3) insert an executive summary in a new document; or (4) hide everything except the executive summary without leaving the document. The first option—highlighting the key points—is a particularly good teaching tool. Figure 6.4 shows the highlighted key information selected by the AutoSummarize tool.

Figure 6.4

Microsoft Word Document Showing AutoSummarize Mark-Up

The Earth's land surfaces are also in motion. For example, the North American continent continues to move west over the Pacific Ocean basin, at a rate roughly equal to the growth of our fingernails. Earthquakes result when plates grind past one another, ride up over one another, collide to make mountains, or split and separate. These movements are known as plate tectonics. Developed within the last 30 years, this explanation has unified the results of centuries of study of our planet, long believed to be unmoving.

Students can use AutoSummarize to summarize, of course, but it has other applications in the writing process. For example, after a student has completed a rough draft, he or she can use the Auto-Summarize tool to see if Word identifies the same main points that the student intended. If the computer and the author disagree on the main points, this might indicate a need for revision.

Note Taking

One of the classroom recommendations for note taking is to use a variety of formats. A format that has a strong impact is combination notes, which employ outlining, webbing, and pictographs in addition to words. Graphic representation has been shown to produce a percentile gain of 39 points in student achievement (Marzano, 1998, p. 74). In the combination notes format, students begin with an inverted *T* on their paper. They record facts and notes on the left side of the page, use drawing or other nonlinguistic representations on the right, and then write a one- or two-sentence summary under the bar of the *T*. In Figure 6.5's example, you see combination notes used during a 1st grade class's discussion of the parts of a computer. The four parts of the computer the teacher discussed are listed on the left side, a drawing of the four parts is on the right, and there's a short sentence at the bottom to summarize the discussion.

It is relatively simple to create combination notes using the draw tools in Word. In the multimedia section that comes later in this

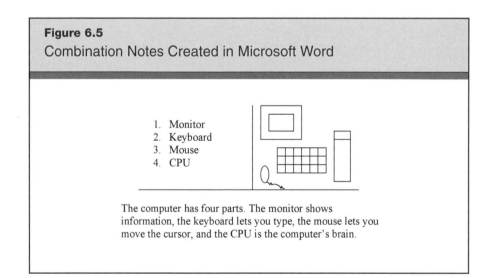

Figure 6.5
Combination Notes Created in Microsoft Word

1. Monitor
2. Keyboard
3. Mouse
4. CPU

The computer has four parts. The monitor shows information, the keyboard lets you type, the mouse lets you move the cursor, and the CPU is the computer's brain.

chapter, we show how combination notes are even easier to create using PowerPoint.

Remember that one of the generalizations from McREL's research on note taking is that the more notes taken, the better, and one of the recommendations for classroom practice is that students should be taught a variety of note-taking formats. Word processing applications help students to take notes quickly and with automatic formatting.

Here's an example. Mr. Ervin, a high school history teacher, wishes to have his U.S. History students take notes as they watch a film on Vietnam protesters. He checks out a laptop cart from the school's library and asks his students to use a word processing program to take notes in an informal outline. The Bullets button in Microsoft Word, for example, makes it easy to create these informal outlines. As students type their notes, they can increase bullet indention by using the Tab key and can decrease indention by hitting Shift + Tab. An excerpt from one of Mr. Ervin's students' notes might look something like this:

- Student Protesters
  - Many people felt strongly that the U.S. should not be in the war.
  - College students were especially opposed, as their age group was most likely to be drafted.
  - Kent State is probably the best-known student protest.
    - Crosby, Stills, Nash, and Young: "Ohio."

○ Organizing and Brainstorming Software

The features in organizing and brainstorming software support distinct ways of enhancing summarizing and note taking.

Summarizing

Using summary frames is one of the explicit recommendations for classroom practice. Summary frames are a series of questions that the teacher asks students, designed to highlight the critical elements of specific kinds of information and texts. *Classroom Instruction That Works* presents six types of summary frames: *narrative, topic-restriction-illustration (T-R-I), definition, argumentation, problem/solution,* and *conversation* (Marzano et al., 2001, p. 35). Inspiration is a great tool to enhance your use of each. Consider the example of Mr. Hernandez, whose biology class will be watching a video on monotremes (egg-laying mammals). To help his students' summarize the video, he decides to use a *definition* frame. A definition frame asks the following questions:

- What is the term to define?
- What is the general category to which the term belongs?
- What are the characteristics that set this apart from other elements in the set?
- What are some types of the item being defined?

Using Inspiration, he creates a template that each student can download to his or her laptop (see Figure 6.6). As the students watch the video, they add information to fill in sections of this definition frame template.

Figure 6.6
Definition Frame Template Created in Inspiration

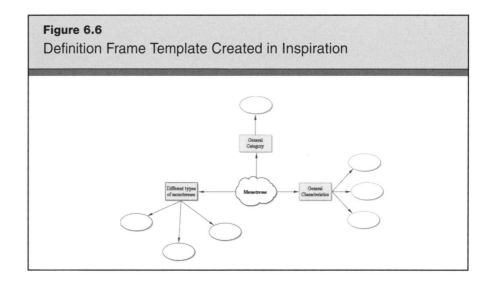

Mr. Hernandez completes his plans: Following the video, the students will meet in pairs to compare their definition frames and make revisions as needed. They'll use these revised definition frames to review for the test at the end of the week, and then place the documents in the teacher's drop box on the server for evaluation and a grade.

During class, Mr. Hernandez finds that some of his students are having difficulty filling out the section of the template on different types of monotremes. He decides to use a second type of summary frame, the *topic-restriction-illustration (T-R-I)* frame to help them. The T-R-I frame presents students with these three guiding questions:

- What is the general topic or statement?
- What information does the author give that narrows or restricts the topic or statement?
- What examples does the author give to illustrate the topic or restriction?

Mr. Hernandez gives the students who are having difficulty in finding different types of monotremes a section of the textbook on monotremes. Using the T-R-I frame's guiding questions, the students are able to determine different types of monotremes and complete the assignment.

Here's another example: Mr. Winslow is teaching his 6th graders a unit titled "Pollution: It's a Dirty Word." After a short lecture about different types of power plants, he shows some videos he has downloaded from United Streaming that depict the pollution from coal-fired plants. He also shows a short video of the nuclear disaster at Chernobyl. The class sees the pollution from coal plants, but students also see the possible problems with nuclear power plants. To help his students summarize their thinking, Mr. Winslow chooses to use a *problem/solution* frame. The problem/solution frame directs students to look at an issue through the lens of these five guiding questions:

1. What is the problem?
2. What is a possible solution?
3. What is another possible solution?
4. What is another possible solution?
5. Which solution has the best chance of succeeding?

Mr. Winslow uses a template from Inspiration's template library: File > Open Template > Thinking Skills > Problem Solution.ist. Shown in Figure 6.7, this template guides students as they work in groups to define the problem and propose possible solutions. It gives them a clear structure for looking at the problem and helps them see that possible solutions might lead to unintended consequences.

Figure 6.7
Problem/Solution Template Created in Inspiration

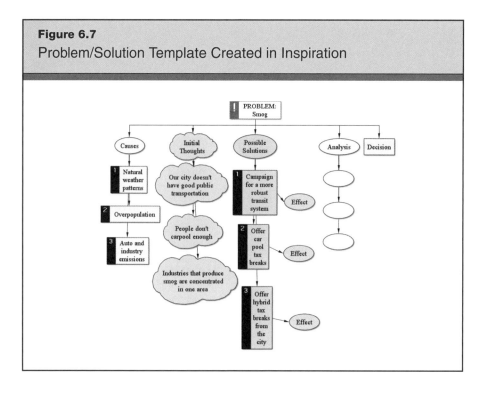

Note Taking

Most teachers insist that their students take notes. After all, how will students study if they don't have good notes? Unfortunately, too few students really understand what it means to take good notes. The classroom recommendations for note taking include using a variety of note-taking formats and giving students teacher-prepared notes. Inspiration has a large number of templates that are terrific aids to teachers and students in the note-taking process.

Recall Ms. Simpson, the 10th grade language arts teacher who used PowerPoint and videos as advance organizers to begin a unit on John Steinbeck's *The Grapes of Wrath*. She then assigned a few chapters of the book for weekend reading. When the students return to school on Monday, she has them sit in base groups (see more on base groups in Chapter 7's discussion of cooperative learning) and discuss the character traits of the main character, Tom Joad. She wants their discussion to focus on the traits that she thinks Steinbeck intentionally developed, so she uses Inspiration to put together some notes to guide the base group conversations. Some students are more comfortable dealing with text than with graphics, so after Ms. Simpson creates the Inspiration document, she clicks File > Transfer to Word Processor and is able to give students both a graphic and an outline version of her teacher-prepared notes. Figure 6.8 illustrates how Ms. Simpson wants her students to focus on the traits of pragmatism, kindness, and being quick to anger. She also guides the students to find specific examples of each trait throughout the book.

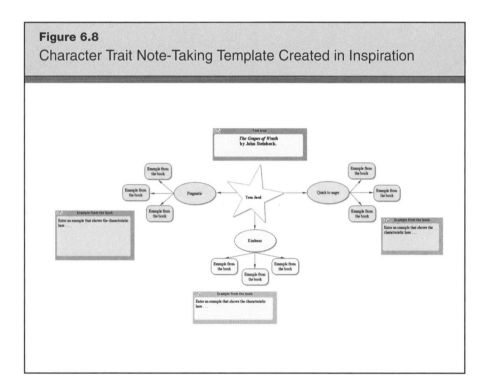

Figure 6.8
Character Trait Note-Taking Template Created in Inspiration

↻ Multimedia

Not only can students create summaries and notes of multimedia content, they can also use multimedia to enhance and present their summaries and notes. For instance, three high school students use a wiki to collaborate on a project where they create a "teaser" for a movie about the life of Julius Caesar. They all take their notes separately during class, but using the wiki, they combine and summarize their notes to create their script. We'll discuss this example further in the upcoming section on communication software.

When students experience multimedia, they sometimes get caught up in the entertainment factor and neglect the critical analysis of the content necessary to create useful notes they can use for further study. When teachers introduce multimedia into their classrooms, they must ensure that students stay focused on distinguishing trivial content from essential content, coalescing minor points into major themes, and personalizing their notes based on their learning styles.

The same is true when students create multimedia summaries: They are often tempted to focus on presentation rather than substance. Obviously, spending lots of time selecting fonts and background colors is not time well spent; identifying and analyzing the essential components of the content is. On the plus side, using multimedia to summarize and take notes is fun, which engages students in the content.

For example, students might interview their grandparents about a historical event or era they lived through. This is a tried and true lesson that teachers have used for many years, but with technology enhancements, it has become the type of project that parents archive with their family keepsakes.

Here's a more specific illustration. Mr. Medina assigns his middle school social studies students to interview senior citizens at a nearby assisted living facility about the civil rights movement. Students videotape the interviews and watch them with their groups when they are back in class. During the viewings, they take notes, discuss the interviews, and summarize the interviews and sort them by common themes. Then they create a "news broadcast" about the civil rights movement, using clips of actual interview footage. Because each group has only three minutes for their news broadcast, it's essential that students apply their summarizing skills to create a product that is concise yet thorough.

In another example, Mrs. Cho wishes to combine moviemaking and the *conversation* summary frame for a character education lesson for her 6th grade students. Her students work in groups of three to videotape a nonviolent bullying scene, then exchange the tapes and go through the steps of a conversation frame:

1. How did the characters greet each other?
2. What questions or topic was insinuated, revealed, or referred to?
3. How did their discussion progress?

4. What was the conclusion?

Using this summary frame, the class is better able to analyze exactly what constitutes "bullying"; they later use their definition to create agreed-upon rules for how to treat each other and other schoolmates.

Another great way to use multimedia to summarize and take notes is with PowerPoint-based combination notes. This two-column format links essential concepts on the left with multimedia enhancements on the right of a PowerPoint slide. Along the bottom of the slide, an overall statement summarizes the combination notes. Figures 6.9 and 6.10 show a teacher's assignment and template.

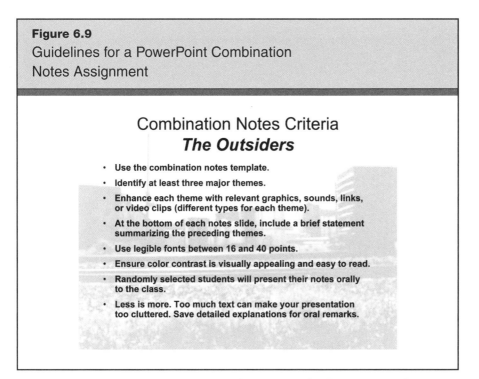

Figure 6.9
Guidelines for a PowerPoint Combination
Notes Assignment

Combination Notes Criteria
The Outsiders

- Use the combination notes template.
- Identify at least three major themes.
- Enhance each theme with relevant graphics, sounds, links, or video clips (different types for each theme).
- At the bottom of each notes slide, include a brief statement summarizing the preceding themes.
- Use legible fonts between 16 and 40 points.
- Ensure color contrast is visually appealing and easy to read.
- Randomly selected students will present their notes orally to the class.
- Less is more. Too much text can make your presentation too cluttered. Save detailed explanations for oral remarks.

Clip art images © 2007 Jupiterimages Corporation.

Figure 6.11 shows an example of a student's use of combination notes to summarize the book *The Outsiders* by S. E. Hinton. Although the images, sound, and video that the student selected might not seem like ones you would choose, the student chose examples that are personally meaningful. This is especially important because the

Figure 6.10
Combination Notes Template Created in PowerPoint

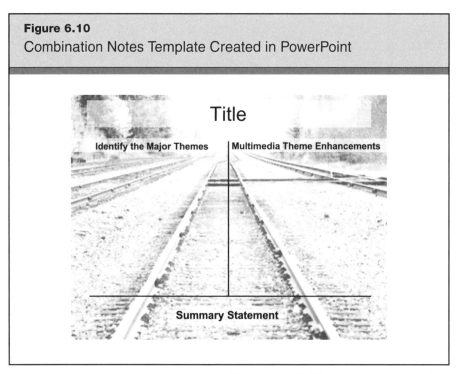

Clip art images © 2007 Jupiterimages Corporation.

Figure 6.11
Combination Notes Created in PowerPoint

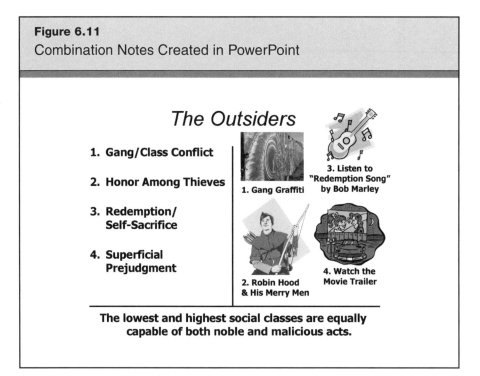

Photograph by Les Chatfield (leslie_chatfield@yahoo.co.uk).
Clip art images © 2007 Jupiterimages Corporation.

notes serve as a personalized tool to help him study and remember the themes in the book.

Note that the students are using an *argumentation* frame for themes. The four elements they have to address are evidence, claim, support, and a qualifier for their theme, using the following questions:

1. *Evidence:* What information does the author present that leads to a claim?

2. *Claim:* What does the author assert is true? What basic statement or claim is the focus of the information?

3. *Support:* What examples or explanations support the claim?

4. *Qualifier:* What restrictions on the claim or evidence counter to the claim is presented?

In this example, the claim is that the lowest and highest social classes are just as capable of noble or malicious acts.

○ Web Resources

Many teachers and students see summarizing and note taking as individual activities, and often they are. However, there are ways to summarize and take notes collaboratively, and there several Web sites that facilitate this:

• NoteStar
http://notestar.4teachers.org

NoteStar allows students to take information from the Web, organize it, and automatically create citations in either MLA or APA style. Teachers can also establish projects and assign individual students sections of the project to complete. This site is designed for students in grades 4–12.

• Google Docs and Spreadsheets
http://docs.google.com

This free resource is an online word processor and spreadsheet editor that can be shared by multiple users. It provides a way for students to work on papers and notes together.

• ThinkFree
www.thinkfree.com

Similar to Google Docs and Spreadsheets, ThinkFree is a free office suite available online. Users can collaborate to prepare documents, spreadsheets, and presentations.

- ThinkTank
http://thinktank.4teachers.org

Designed for grades 3–8, ThinkTank allows students to use online tools to zero in on a project topic. The site is organized as a kind of narrative frame in that it uses a series of questions to prompt users as they develop the project. This site also allows integration with NoteStar as students begin work on their project.

- Cornell Notes
http://cssdesigns.com/learningtoolbox/cornell.html

Many schools use Cornell Notes as a school or districtwide strategy. This site, from the Learning Toolbox, provides a good tutorial on making Cornell Notes.

- Rochester Institute of Technology
www.rit.edu/%7E369www/college_programs/lng_pwr/lecture_notetaking_main_page.htm

The Rochester Institute of Technology has a very strong resource page designed to help students, especially at the high school level, with summarizing and note-taking strategies. The section on "Verbal Cues to Organization" would be especially helpful to students in thinking about nonlinguistic representation in combination notes.

- Summary Frames
www.d214.org/shard/depts./staffsupport/SchoolImprovement/docs/sumframespower.pdf

Township High School in Arlington Heights, Illinois, has a very complete resource for understanding and using summary frames.

○ Communication Software

Although e-mail and group folders on a server can certainly support summarizing and note taking, there are new tools that provide much more intuitive and seamless ways for students to collaborate as they take notes and summarize. Collaborative Web-based tools such as wikis and blogs allow groups to share resources, edit Web pages, and easily find and categorize information by means of "tags," or short descriptors of resources. In this section, we show the role that wikis and blogs can play in collaborative summarizing and note taking.

Wikis

Mr. Simmons, a 10th grade English teacher, is wrapping up his class's study of Shakespeare's *Julius Caesar*. For a final project, which will serve to assess his students' understanding of the play, he asks students to make a short movie trailer—a preview-style advertisement—for a movie about the life of Julius Caesar. Before giving the assignment, he creates a rubric by modifying Rubistar's Multimedia criteria and grading on the qualities of voice, soundtrack, economy, historical accuracy, and enticement. The assignment follows:

> Create a teaser (trailer) for an imaginary movie about the life of Julius Caesar. You can use live motion, clay animation, cut-out animation, or drawn animation. Your movie needs to include voiceover narration, a soundtrack, and scenes from Caesar's life as depicted in Shakespeare's play. You may work independently or in self-selected groups of up to three people. See our class Web site to access the rubric for more detailed information about this assignment.

A group of students—Jake, Shantel, and Dion—decide to do a live-action trailer. The first thing they need to do is combine the individual notes that they took throughout the class's study of the play into a collective set of notes. Next, they'll need to summarize these collective notes into the beginning of a script for their project. They decide to use the Peanut Butter Wiki (http://pbwiki.com) to help them collaborate.

PBWiki has a number of easy-to-understand tutorials to help the students quickly learn how to create and personalize a wiki. Following the guidelines available, Jake creates the wiki (http://caesar.pbwiki.com) and copies and pastes his notes from various lectures onto a page that he creates and names CaesarBio. He also finds a picture of a bust of Caesar on the Wikipedia Web site and copies it to his page. Shantel and Dion read his posted notes and copy and paste some of their own, resulting in a collaborative page of facts about Julius Caesar.

In the wiki that Jake began, Shantel creates three new pages: Resources, Assignment, and Storyboard. She also adds a sidebar for easy navigation. On the Resources page, she links to Wikipedia and her own del.icio.us account, which contains her saved Web links that she has tagged as "Caesar." This allows the group to easily share resources as they write their script. Next, Dion posts the original assignment from Mr. Simmons so that they all can stay focused on the topic. He also copies and pastes Mr. Simmons's rubric on a separate page.

Now, to the project itself. Shantel suggests that they first type a script and then work on the storyboard. Jake agrees, so all three students begin to edit and shape their trailer's script. The students are able to work on the script separately from home, together during their lunch hour or study hall, and either individually or collaboratively in the school media center before and after school. The wiki serves as a common area for them to take notes, summarize information, and plan and carry out their project. If Mr. Simmons or any member of the group wishes to see changes made throughout the process, they are available for viewing in the "history" of each wiki page, along with an indication of who saved each change. Most wikis, including PBWiki, have this feature.

Before assigning this project, Mr. Simmons had taught his students the six different summary frames that are discussed in detail in *Classroom Instruction That Works* (Marzano et al., 2001). To help them summarize their teaser, he suggests that they use a narrative summary frame. This, he explains, will work well for the play because it will guide them through questions that commonly relate to fiction and help them identify the characters, setting, initiating event, internal response, goal, consequence, and resolution of the play. For their trailer, Jake, Shantel, and Dion decide to omit the consequence and resolution so that it won't "give away" the end of the movie.

Blogs

Blogs provide a very effective way to implement the strategy of *reciprocal teaching*. This highly structured form of peer teaching has four components: (1) summarizing, (2) questioning, (3) clarifying, and (4) predicting. After the students have read a section independently, one student *summarizes* the information for the class. Other members of the class or the teacher may help during this process. The student then asks *questions* to the class in order to highlight important sections of the text. Then the same student asks classmates to *clarify* confusing information. Finally, the student asks for *predictions* about what will follow the passage they just read.

The reciprocal teaching format can be used not just with reading and face-to-face conversation, but also with Web-based educational movies and blogs. For example, Ms. Holt, a 4th grade teacher, wishes to employ reciprocal teaching as her students are learning about different forms of energy. Blogs provide the means for students to use the strategy of reciprocal teaching but allow time for more in-depth conversation that can extend beyond the allotted time in the classroom. Ms. Holt logs on to BrainPOP, and the entire class watches the short, Flash-based movie *Forms of Energy*. As they are watching, she types the vocabulary terms from the movie on a blog: *potential, kinetic, chemical, electrical, light, mechanical, thermal,* and *nuclear.* She then selects Jonah to lead the class's discussion on the blog.

Jonah signs on to the blog and begins by *summarizing* what he understood from the movie: that energy can come from a variety of places, and that potential energy is stored energy while kinetic energy involves motion. He then types in some *questions* about each of the types of energy for his classmates to answer. By the next day, they respond with their understanding and come up with several examples of each type of energy. They are able to read these together as a class using a projector. Ms. Holt is thrilled with the level of conversation that her students are having.

On the second day, discussion leader Jonah *asks for clarification* on nuclear energy. This seems confusing for all, so they watch that segment of the *Forms of Energy* video again. Ms. Holt also clarifies nuclear energy by posting on the blog and receives numerous "a-ha!" responses. Finally, Jonah *makes the prediction* that they will next learn about which forms of energy are safer and cheaper. He notices that one of the videos related to *Forms of Energy* on BrainPOP is *Fossil Fuels,* so he also *makes the prediction* that they will be learning about how fossil fuels are used to create energy.

The blog serves as an archive of class discussions for later review and as a part of their assessment. Ms. Holt shares the blog's Web address with parents, who enjoy getting a peek at the conversations taking place in the classroom.

7

COOPERATIVE LEARNING

The instructional strategy of *cooperative learning* focuses on having students interact with each other in groups in ways that enhance their learning. When students work in cooperative groups, they make sense of, or construct meaning for, new knowledge by interacting with others (Johnson, Johnson, & Stanne, 2000.) As Thomas Friedman notes in *The World Is Flat* (2005), we are living in a time when learning and innovation are increasingly global. To be prepared for the fast-paced, virtual workplace that they will inherit, today's students need to be able to learn and produce cooperatively.

McREL's research on cooperative learning supports the following generalizations:

GENERALIZATIONS

1. Organizing groups based on ability levels should be done sparingly.
2. Cooperative learning groups should be rather small in size.
3. Cooperative learning should be used consistently and systematically but should not be overused.

Based on these findings, we have four recommendations for classroom practice:

RECOMMENDATIONS

1. Use a variety of criteria to group students.
2. Use informal, formal, and base groups.
3. Keep the groups to a manageable size.
4. Combine cooperative learning with other classroom structures.

It is helpful to use informal groups for short, impromptu activities that take no longer than a few minutes. There are a variety of structures teachers might use, and many are as simple as announcing, "Numbered heads together" or "Turn to someone sitting next to you." For formal groups, however, teachers should intentionally design assignments to include these five basic components:

1. *Positive interdependence* (sink or swim together)

2. *Face-to-face, promotive interaction* (helping each other to learn, applauding efforts and success)

3. *Individual and group accountability* (each of us has to contribute to the group achieving its goal)

4. *Interpersonal and small-group skills* (communication, trust, leadership, decision making, conflict resolution)

5. *Group processing* (reflecting on how well the team is functioning and how to function even better)

Base groups are long-term groups, created to provide students with support throughout a semester or school year. Base groups help build trust, camaraderie, and teamwork, and they are useful for checking homework and completing tasks and other routines. They also can be used for planning and participating in activities like field trips.

Technology can play a unique and vital role in cooperative learning by facilitating group collaboration, providing structure for group tasks, and allowing members of groups to communicate even if they are not working face to face. It can help us realize the hope of schools as places that serve students anytime, anywhere and facilitate their growth into lifelong learners. Studies show that there is a modest increase in effect size when students use technology collaboratively (Urquhart & McIver, 2005). In this section, we show how *multimedia, Web resources,* and *communication software* can facilitate cooperative learning.

○ Multimedia

Student-created multimedia is a natural environment for cooperative learning. Creating a video is a complex task that requires many roles and responsibilities. By nature, both multimedia projects and cooperative learning groups require attention to detail in the planning process. When these types of activities go astray in the classroom, it is often due to inadequate up-front preparation. As we discussed in Chapter 4's focus on advance organizers, rubrics help students understand what is expected of them and how their participation will be evaluated. While this is important in any learning activity, it is especially important in cooperative learning activities. Figure 7.1 shows a rubric that Ms. Ortiz, a middle school teacher, distributes to her students at the beginning of a two-week movie project about the lives of famous mathematicians. Notice that in this example, she is having her students work in formal cooperative groups. To follow the classroom recommendation for cooperative learning, in other lessons she will want to vary the grouping to include individual work, pairs, base groups, and informal groups.

After introducing the project and providing the students with a project rubric, Ms. Ortiz turns her attention to student roles and responsibilities. The class works in small groups of three or four to create short movies focused on curricular topics. She creates a chart like the one shown in Figure 7.2 as an advance organizer to guide students in the process and assigns each student two or three of the responsibilities. Some of the tasks require just one student, while other roles, such as researchers, journalists, and actors, require multiple students. The students are allowed to work on the project every other class period for two weeks, with homework assigned for their basic computation work.

At the end of the two weeks, the students view each others' movies and take notes as necessary. Together, they learn about Pythagoras, Euclid, Fibonacci, Pascal, Archimedes, and Banneker, and about how the work that these men did relates to our use of mathematics

Figure 7.1
Rubric for a Cooperative Multimedia Project

Multimedia Project: Curriculum Movie
Teacher: Ms. Ortiz
Student Name:

CATEGORY	4	3	2	1
Content	Covers topic in depth with details and examples. Subject knowledge is excellent.	Includes essential knowledge about the topic. Subject knowledge appears to be good.	Includes essential information about the topic but there are 1–2 factual errors.	Content is minimal OR there are several factual errors.
Rough Draft	Rough draft is ready for review on due date. Student shares draft with a peer and makes edits based on feedback.	Rough draft is ready for review on due date. Student shares draft with a peer and peer makes edits.	Rough draft not ready for review on due date. Student provides feedback and/or edits for peer.	Rough draft not ready for review on due date. Student does not participate in reviewing draft of peer.
Organization	Content is well organized; headings or bulleted lists group related material.	Content is logically organized for the most part.	Headings or bulleted lists group material, but the overall organization of topics appears flawed.	There is no clear or logical organizational structure, just lots of facts.
Storyboard	Storyboard includes all required elements as well as a few additional elements.	Storyboard includes all required elements and one additional element.	Storyboard includes all required elements.	One or more required elements are missing from the storyboard.
Originality	Product shows a large amount of original thought. Ideas are creative and inventive.	Product shows some original thought. Work shows new ideas and insights.	Product uses other people's ideas (giving credit), but there is little evidence of original thinking.	Product uses other people's ideas but does not give them credit.
Attractiveness	Student makes excellent use of video, graphics, sounds, and effects to enhance the presentation.	Student makes good use of video, graphics, sounds, and effects to enhance to the presentation.	Student uses video, graphics, sounds, and effects, but occasionally these detract from the presentation content.	Student uses video, graphics, sounds, and effects, but these often distract from the presentation content.

Figure 7.2
Group Roles in a Cooperative Multimedia Project

Role	Role or Task Description	Student Name(s)
Researcher (2)	Will research the topic and meet with a teacher in that content area to be sure information is accurate.	
Scriptwriter (2)	Will take the research provided by the researchers and write a script for the movie. (The teacher must approve a storyboard before the script is finalized. A content area teacher will review the final draft of script for accuracy.) The script will be in play format and will indicate all resources needed and the settings where the action takes place.	
Journalist (1 or 2)	Will provide any on-camera interviews with experts. Journalists will use the provided research to write interview questions that will get additional information needed for the movie.	
Tech Expert (1 or 2)	Will provide help with all technology (e.g., iMovie, GarageBand, and GraphicConverter).	
Project Coordinator (1)	Will work with the team to build a project timeline and then will monitor all project activities. Responsible for coordinating resources with other teams. (Remember that other teams will be using the video cameras.)	
Camera Operator (1 or 2)	Will be responsible for checking out, using, and properly returning video cameras and tripods.	
Actor (as needed)	Will use the provided script to bring the movie to life. Actors should be expressive and show appropriate excitement but stay within the script.	

today. In this way, the students are not only working together in cooperative groups to create the movies, but are actually participating in cooperative teaching.

○ Web Resources

Cooperative learning is not so much learning to cooperate as it is cooperating to learn (Wong & Wong, 1998). Rapid advances in network infrastructure and bandwidth in our schools have made this approach more feasible than ever. Now students can collaborate through the Web with other students in their school, subject experts, and multiuser game players. They can even collaborate across the globe!

Web-enabled collaborative learning has evolved dramatically from its initial use as a simple way for students to look up information together on Web sites. As we discuss in the upcoming section on communication software, the Web has become much more than an electronic reference book; today, it's a thriving medium for collaboration in business, education, and our personal lives.

One of the best-known and most successful Web collaborations is the JASON Project (www.jasonproject.org), an organization focused on engaging students in hands-on scientific discovery. JASON's standards-based Expeditions curricula are geared to students in grades 4–9. With the help of multimedia tools and Internet broadcasting technology, participating students become part of a virtual research community, accompanying real researchers in real time as they explore everything from oceans to rainforests to polar regions to volcanoes. The live expedition broadcasts are available via KU Band satellite dish and via the National Geographic Channel. Regional JASON network sites typically offer access, at their own locations, to the live Expedition broadcasts. Students can also take advantage of all of the online activities available through Team JASON Online.

The Web gives students access to experts in nearly any subject area, from Nobel Prize winners to best-selling authors to Olympic athletes. There are many "Ask an Expert" Web sites devoted specifically to answering student questions. One such example is the question section of the National Science Digital Library found at http://nsdl. org/asknsdl. Alternatively, students can correspond via e-mail with experts from universities or industries as part of a particular project. There is nothing quite like getting expert advice straight from the professionals in the field. For instance, a student who has a question about wind turbines might contact the National Wind Technology Center at www.nrel.gov/wind/nwtc.html; the site administrator will route that question to an actual mechanical engineer who does cutting-edge research on wind energy. The engineer will reply directly to the student using the e-mail address submitted with the question.

Keypals

Communication with students in other cities, states, and countries broadens the perspective of students and challenges them to learn about other cultures, languages, and issues throughout the world. The expansion of global telecommunication networks has made this possible in even some of the world's most remote regions. Students can use e-mail to collaborate with students in other classes in your school, or they can correspond and collaborate with "keypals" (e-mail pen pals) from far away. There are many examples of Web sites that facilitate correspondence and project-based learning between students and other communities. Monitored to ensure effective communications for educational purposes, these sites are just as safe as traditional postcard-type projects. Here are some of the best:

- ePALS
www.epals.com/

This is the Internet's largest community of collaborative classrooms engaged in cross-cultural exchanges, project sharing, and language learning.

- Keypals Club International
www.worldkids.net/clubs/kci

A free place for young people, teachers, and students to locate and correspond with other youth and students, the service provides an easy-to-use interface and database to quickly locate and contact a student or a class from around the world.

- Intercultural E-mail Classroom Connections (IECC)
www.iecc.org

IECC is dedicated to helping teachers connect with other teachers to arrange intercultural e-mail connections between their students. Also, IECC-INTERGEN helps teachers and their classrooms create intergenerational partnerships with volunteers over age 50.

WebQuests

WebQuests are inquiry-oriented activities that allow students in a class or from multiple locations to work together to learn about a particular subject or to tackle a particular project or problem.

WebQuests are designed to use learners' time well, to focus on using information rather than looking for it, and to support learners' thinking at the levels of analysis, synthesis, and evaluation (Dodge & March, 1995). A well-designed WebQuest task is practical, engaging, and elicits student thinking. It provides a goal to channel student energies and also clarifies the teacher's learning objectives. Here are some Web sites that will help you find or design effective WebQuests:

- San Diego State University's WebQuest
http://webquest.org

This is the original WebQuest site. It is still among the best resources for learning about WebQuests, finding exemplary models, and creating WebQuests.

- WebQuest Taskonomy
http://webquest.sdsu.edu/taskonomy.html

Here, you'll find a taxonomy of the 12 most common types of Web-Quest tasks.

- A WebQuest About WebQuests
http://webquest.sdsu.edu/materials.htm

This URL links to an exercise that's a useful introduction to the WebQuest concept. Designed for educators working in teams, it prompts you to examine five WebQuests from four different points of view. There are several versions of the exercise tailored to teachers in different grade levels and subjects.

- Teacher WebQuest Generator
http://teacherweb.com/TWQuest.htm

This is an interactive WebQuest wizard that allows you to select from a variety of themed pages and fill in the form with your information. The WebQuest is stored on the TeacherWeb site and can be edited using your password. Students can view the page using the direct URL.

- Instant Projects
http://instantprojects.org

This is a great site for creating WebQuests, portfolios, and teacher Web sites, and it's all free.

An excellent example of a WebQuest designed to be a cooperative learning experience is Tom March's *Searching for China* (www.kn. pacbell.com/wired/China/ChinaQuest.html). It is a scenario in which the United States government assembles a special fact-finding team that will travel to China and return with an accurate and informed concept of the country, its people, and their culture. Instead of sending only diplomats or politicians, the government forms a team that includes people from very different backgrounds so that the facts they find will be enriched by differing perspectives. This WebQuest incorporates many of the fundamentals of collaborative learning, such as positive interdependence, individual and group accountability, interpersonal and small-group skills, and group processing. A useful collaboration rubric for the project is available at http://edweb. sdsu.edu/triton/tidepoolunit/Rubrics/collrubric.html.

Web Site Creation

Building a Web site can be a very enriching collaborative experience for students. For example, Mrs. Cox in Williamsburg, Virginia, teaches her students to work in teams to build a Web site in four phases. The main goal is for students to develop a multipage Web site based on their research of a city. The problem the students solve focuses on how to attract businesses, tourists, and new residents to the city. The students have an authentic audience, as they e-mail the finished product to their chosen city's Chamber of Commerce. The five phases of the project are as follows:

- Phase I: Research a city.
- Phase II: Create a multimedia presentation about that city.
- Phase III: Create a multipage Web site for that city.
- Phase IV: Present a proposal to the rest of the class focused on increasing the city's tourism, drawing new residents, and bringing in new businesses.
- Phase V: Contact the city's Chamber of Commerce to announce the Web site creation and seek feedback.

Figure 7.3 is an illustration of Phase V: the text of e-mail message sent by one of the student team leaders to the London Chamber of Commerce. You can browse the group's Web site at www.freewebs. com/classcox.

Figure 7.3
Element of a Cooperative Web Site Creation Project

Dear London Chamber of Commerce,

I am [Group Leader's Name], a student at Berkeley Middle School in Williamsburg, Virginia, USA. Over a three-week time period, my team and I have studied London and made a PowerPoint presentation about the city. We are beginning to create a Web site on London as an assignment. We have thought of some creative ways to convey important information. I thought you might like to see a draft of the Web site we are creating.

We have tried to make the site interesting and eye catching, and we have included some incentives for people to return to the site. We hope to launch it at http://www.freewebs.com/classcox/ as soon as it is completed.

Part of our class assignment is to ask experts on the city we are studying for feedback on the Web site we are creating. We hope that you will be able to participate and look at our Web site design. I have included everything as an attachment. Microsoft Publisher is the software you will need to run the Web site. Please let us know what modifications we can make and what results we should expect.

Thanks so much. We hope to hear from you soon.

Sincerely,

[Signed Name]

Over the past decade, it has become easier and easier to make Web sites. Today, there are many free and inexpensive software programs for Web site creation. Here are a few:

- iWeb
www.apple.com/ilife/iweb

Designed for Macintosh operating systems, iWeb provides a way to create Web sites and blogs—complete with podcasts, photos, and movies—and get them online fast. An array of Web templates makes design a simple matter of dragging and dropping.

- Microsoft Office Publisher
http://office.microsoft.com/en-us/publisher

Publisher helps you create professional-looking Web sites that are customized for your needs. Publisher provides enhanced features for creating, editing, publishing, and updating Web sites.

- TOWeb
www.lauyan.com/en/tw-home

This is easy-to-use software that enables individuals without preexisting Web designing skills to quickly create a Web site or a blog.

- SiteSpinner
www.virtualmechanics.com

This is another simple-to-use yet powerful drag-and-drop editor for quickly creating sophisticated Web sites without the need to know HTML or another programming language. Use one of the included templates to get started, or begin with your own design.

- Cool Page
www.coolpage.com

Designed for Windows operating systems, this Web page design tool allows you to create a page simply by dragging and dropping objects into a layout. By pushing a publish button, you can automatically upload your site to the Internet.

Collaborative Organizing

Students and teachers can collaborate over the Web by logging on to sites that allow them to share and edit calendars, bookmark and share Web links, and create online learning communities. These Web resources are often referred to as "Web 2.0" or the "Read/Write Web" because users are able to collaborate and share information online.

Shared calendars. With shared calendars, students can work from home or from various locales within the school and still organize the activities within their group.

Even better, students can provide teachers with access to these shared calendars for progress monitoring. Here are some of the more popular calendar-hosting sites:

- Yahoo! Calendar
http://calendar.yahoo.com

With a free Yahoo! account, you can set up a group calendar with many useful features.

- Google Calendar
www.google.com/googlecalendar/tour.html

With a free Google account, you can set up a group calendar with lots of user-friendly features.

- Calendars Net
www.calendars.net

This is a free, interactive Web calendar-hosting service, where you and anyone you choose can post events that will be visible and printable by whomever you choose, or everyone.

Shared bookmarking. Before the Web supported the quick and easy sharing of Web links, many teachers used to log onto each computer in a computer lab and bookmark the sites they wanted students to go to for a project. Although this kept the students on task with the appropriate Web sites, it was very time consuming for the teacher. Now all a teacher has to do is bookmark her best resources on a social bookmarking site and make one link to it that stays on the computers all year. Students can use the teacher site at home or at school without having to remember a lot of URLs. For cooperative learning projects, students can set up their own social bookmarking sites to categorize (tag) Web sites and share them with others in their group. Here are some of the more popular social bookmarking Web sites:

- del.icio.us
http://del.icio.us

With del.icio.us, you can keep your favorite Web sites, music, books, and more in a place where you can always find them; share your favorites with students and colleagues; and discover new and interesting things by browsing popular and related items.

- Blinklist
www.blinklist.com

Blinklist lets students import and manage bookmarks, create watch lists to see what others in their group are discovering online, and follow the wisdom of the group member's most selected resources.

- Kaboodle
www.kaboodle.com

With Kaboodle, users can "collect" anything found on the Web, from photos to blogs, with one click; compare and share everything on one page; and discover interesting things on pages of like-minded users.

Course management. In addition to blogs and wikis discussed in earlier sections, teachers can create online learning communities for their students through Web-enabled course management system (CMS) programs. These services allow teachers to securely share resources, facilitate online discussions, and post information. Students share ideas, communicate as a group, and learn collectively. Many universities use these services regularly. We list some common online services here:

- Moodle
http://moodle.org/

This is a free CMS—an open source software package designed to help educators create effective online learning communities.

- The Global Schoolhouse
www.globalschoolnet.org/GSH/

The Global Schoolhouse is the original virtual meeting place where educators, students, parents, and community members can collaborate, interact, develop, publish, and discover learning resources.

- Blackboard
www.blackboard.com

The Blackboard Academic Suite enables institutions to access any learning resource at any time from any place.

Web-Enabled Multiplayer Simulation Games

The advent of multiplayer computer games has opened a new avenue of interaction: allowing individuals to interact with other individuals simultaneously through a computer game interface. The difference between these Web-enabled games and typical multiplayer computer games is that the Web-enabled ones allow human-to-human interaction through a simulated computer interface over the Internet rather than *simulating* that interaction through artificial intelligence within the game program. In other words, the interface, surroundings, characters, situations, and challenges are simulated, but the interactions are human to human and real. As the idea of cooperative learning revolves around the concept of students interacting with each other for a common purpose in learning, it's logical to conclude that well-designed multiplayer computer games would lend themselves to facilitating cooperative learning, provided that they are used properly (Lobel, 2006). Indeed, according to Kriz and Eberle (2004), "Gaming simulation is an interactive learning environment that makes it possible to cope with complex authentic situations that are close to reality. At the same time, gaming simulation represents a form of cooperative learning through teamwork" (p. 6).

Revolution (http://educationarcade.org/revolution) is an excellent example of a simulation game designed for collaborative learning. A multiplayer 3D game, Revolution can be played over the Web or within a networked environment. Participants navigate the space of a town, interact with other players and townspeople, and have the opportunity to act in and react to various events that foreshadow the coming of the American Revolution. It includes a narrative component to draw the players into a world of actual historical events. Players also improvise their own stories based on the resources available to them and on the choices they make in real time as the game unfolds. Because the game is networked, players collaborate, debate, and compete, all within a simulation that maintains historical suspension of disbelief with graphic and behavioral accuracy.

Here are some other great games designed to educate collaboratively, along with recommended team-building exercises and rubrics for collaborative work:

- Girls Inc. Team Up
www.girlsinc.org/gc/page.php?id=6.2

This is an elementary problem-solving game in which a team of girls, each of whom has a unique ability, needs to solve spatial puzzles.

- Civilization III
www.civ3.com/ptw_features.cfm

Sid Meier's Civilization is one of the most successful strategy game series ever created. This game lets multiple players match wits against history's greatest leaders as they employ exploration, construction, diplomacy, and conquest to build and rule an empire to stand the test of time.

- Building Homes of Our Own
www.homesofourown.org

This is an interactive teaching tool for middle and high school. The simulation presents a macro view of the entire home-building process, from site selection to final sale. Students collect information, solve problems, and make choices as they build a 3D home.

- Jigsaw Classroom
www.jigsaw.org

This is the official Web site of the jigsaw classroom, a cooperative learning technique that reduces conflict among schoolchildren, promotes better learning, improves student motivation, and increases enjoyment of the learning experience.

- The University of Wisconsin, Stout
www.uwstout.edu/soe/profdev/rubrics.shtml

Several rubrics related to cooperative learning are available here.

- NASA Cooperative Learning Rubric
http://whyfiles.larc.nasa.gov/text/educators/tools/eval/coop_rubric.html

This is an excellent, ready-to-use rubric on cooperative learning.

○ Communication Software

Now more than ever, technology allows students to collaborate on projects without the constraints of time or geography. Because we have already discussed blogs and wikis at length, we will not go into them in detail here, but as our previous examples have illustrated, both blogs and wikis provide the means for students to communicate and share ideas as they work cooperatively.

What we will focus on in this section is on how a teacher might pair instant messaging and Voice over IP (VoIP) with the afore-mentioned communication software to expand formal cooperative learning experiences. Combining VoIP with sites that facilitate user-content sharing—such as instant messaging for quick chats, blogs for discussions, wikis for collaborative note taking, Google Calendar for sharing dates, and del.icio.us for sharing Web resources—facilitates powerful collaboration at any time of day and from any geographical location.

Here's an illustration. Think back to Chapter 6's example of the three high school students who were combining their notes on Pea-nut Butter Wiki to create a teaser for a movie about Julius Caesar. The wiki allowed Jake, Shantel, and Dion to collectively summarize their notes and draft a script. Now, they are ready to make some decisions about when and where to film and who will play which role.

They decide to log onto Skype (www.skype.com), a service that allows multiple users to talk for free, regardless of location, through their computer. After creating Skype accounts and installing a Webcam for the microphone, they agree to meet virtually at 7:00 the next evening. Shantel is able to participate from her laptop, even though she is in another state visiting relatives. As the conversation takes place, they add notes to Skype's chat feature about who has which responsibilities. They are able to save the chat for future refer-ence. They also can send links to each other as they talk, allowing everyone to see the same resources at the same time. Finally, they create a project calendar using Google Calendar (http://calendar.google.com) so that everyone can see due dates and meeting times.

For more information about user-content sharing on the Web and the impact that it is having on education, you may want to read Bryan Alexander's 2006 article "Web 2.0: A New Wave of Innovation for Teaching and Learning?"

8

REINFORCING EFFORT

People attribute success to different sources: to their own innate abilities, to the assistance of others, to luck, and to effort. Of these possible attributions, the fourth, *effort,* is the wisest choice for someone who intends to achieve success or maintain it, as it is the only one within an individual's control. Have you ever heard the saying that "success comes in cans; failure in can'ts"? Its originator must have recognized that effort is the most important factor in achievement. Research shows that the level of belief in self-efficacy plays a strong role in motivation for learning and achievement (Schunk, 2003). The instructional strategy of *reinforcing effort* enhances students' understanding of the relationship between effort and achievement by addressing their attitudes and beliefs about learning.

McREL's research on reinforcing effort supports the following generalizations:

GENERALIZATIONS

1. Not all students realize the importance of believing in effort.
2. Students can learn to operate from a belief that effort pays off even if they do not initially have this belief.

Based on these findings, we have two recommendations for classroom practice:

RECOMMENDATIONS

1. Explicitly teach students about the importance of effort.
2. Have students keep track of their effort and achievement.

Technology makes it easier for students and teachers to track the effects of effort and facilitates more immediate feedback. In this section, we show how *spreadsheet software* and *data collection tools* support the instructional strategy of reinforcing effort by helping students to chart the relationship between effort and achievement—one of the classroom recommendations.

○ Spreadsheet Software

The research tells us that not all students realize the importance of effort. Many attribute their success or failure to external factors. Many of us have heard a struggling mathematics student say something like, "I'm just not good at math. My mom wasn't good at math either." When a student makes a connection between academic successes with factors outside of his or her control—things like heredity, gender, or race—it's easy to develop a defeatist attitude. After all, why bother if you know that you just aren't capable because of your genes?

Some students also see friends who are successful and attribute their success to outside factors. They might even have the misconception that people of a certain background excel in a particular curricular area. By relying on a stereotype, these students ignore the effort other students put into doing well. The research indicates, however, that students can change their beliefs and make a connection between effort and achievement.

One easy way to help students make the connection between effort and achievement is by using a spreadsheet like Microsoft Excel. The first step in the process is to find or create a rubric that gives students a clear idea of what effort looks like. Figure 8.1 shows an effort rubric created by Ms. Powell, a 5th grade teacher.

Figure 8.1
Effort Rubric

CATEGORY	4 – Proficient	3 – Meets Standard	2 – Emerging	1 – Not Acceptable
Class Notes	I take neat notes, keep them neatly organized in a binder, and refer to them every day when doing class work and homework.	I take neat notes, keep them neatly organized in a binder, and usually refer to them often when doing class work and homework.	I take notes, but they are messy or unorganized; I use them occasionally when doing class work and homework.	I often do not take notes or do not keep notes; I almost never refer to notes when doing class work and homework.
Attention	I pay attention in class, listen carefully to the teacher's questions, and focus on the class work at least 95% of the time.	I pay attention in class, listen to the teacher's questions, and focus on the class work 80–95% of the time.	I pay attention in class most of the time. If I am called on, I often know the question the teacher is asking. I focus on the class work 70–80% of the time.	I am off task more than 70% of the time, not listening to instruction. If I am called on, I usually don't know the question, and I don't focus on the class work.
Participation	I ask at least 2 questions a day and volunteer at least 2 answers a day when offered the opportunity, even if I'm not sure my answers are right.	I ask 1 question per day and volunteer 1 answer per day when offered the opportunity, but usually only when I'm certain of being right.	I ask 1–4 questions per week and offer to answer questions 1–4 times per week, but only when I'm certain of being right.	I rarely ask questions or volunteer answers.
Homework	I attempt all problems on every homework assignment, even if I think some of my answers might be incorrect. I refer to class notes while doing homework	I attempt all problems on homework 4 nights per week, even if I think some of my answers might be incorrect. I usually refer to class notes while doing homework.	I attempt most homework problems but not those that seem difficult or confusing. I miss several homework assignments each week and occasionally use notes often when doing homework.	I miss many homework assignments and skip many answers, particularly those problems that appear long or difficult. I almost never refer to class notes when doing homework.
Studying	I begin studying for a test as soon as it is announced. I study class notes for at least 10 minutes per day every day until the test, and attempt 2–3 practice problems.	I begin studying for a test 3–5 days before the test. I study class notes for 5–10 minutes per day every day until the test, and attempt 1–2 practice problems.	I begin studying for a test 2 days before the test. I study class notes for 5–10 minutes each day, and do not attempt practice problems.	I study for the test the night before only. I study class notes sometimes and do not attempt practice problems.

After Ms. Powell reviews the rubric with her students and is sure they all have an understanding of each category, she asks them to log on to the class network and open a blank spreadsheet that she created ahead of time (see Figure 8.2).

Figure 8.2
Effort/Achievement Spreadsheet Template
Created in Microsoft Excel

Category	Week 1	Week 2	Week 3	Week 4
Class Notes				
Attention				
Participation				
Homework				
Studying				
Total Effort				
Grade				

To set up an effort/achievement spreadsheet like his, follow these steps:

1. In Microsoft Excel, type the categories in the first column and label the next four columns (Week 1 through Week 4). Add rows for Total Effort and Grades.

2. Format the spreadsheet to perform automatic calculations by clicking on the Total Effort cell for "Week 1" and typing =SUM(B2:B7). This tells the spreadsheet to add all the numbers in the cells from B2 through B7.

3. Copy that cell and paste it into the Total Effort columns for Week 2, Week 3, and Week 4.

As Ms. Powell's students begin their four-week unit on decimals, they also begin a project on effort and achievement, using the effort rubric to assess themselves honestly on their preparation for their weekly mathematics test. Each Friday, right before they take their test, students open their spreadsheets and enter their rubric scores for the appropriate week. The following Monday, when they get their mathematics tests back, they enter their grades into their spread-sheets. Figure 8.3 shows one student's spreadsheet after the final week.

Figure 8.3

Completed Effort/Achievement Spreadsheet

Category	Week 1	Week 2	Week 3	Week 4
Class Notes	2	1	3	3
Attention	2	1	3	4
Participation	2	2	3	3
Homework	2	2	3	4
Studying	2	2	3	3
Total Effort	11	9	16	19
Grade	10	7	12.5	15

Grade Scale		
A = 20	C+ = 12	D = 5
A– = 19	C = 10	D– = 4
B+ = 17	C– = 9	F = 0
B = 15	D+ = 7	

With their completed spreadsheets open on their laptops, the students follow Ms. Powell's instructions to highlight the rows for Total Effort and Grade and to go to Insert > Chart to select the chart style that they think will make the best sense of the data. A few students select a column chart similar to Figure 8.4.

By looking at the chart, students can clearly see the relation between their effort and grades they earned on their tests. Of course, this exercise alone won't change all of Ms. Powell's students' thinking about effort and achievement. Students need consistent and system-atic exposure to teaching strategies like this one in order to really grasp the impact that effort can have on their achievement.

Here's another method to consider. Mr. Rodriguez, another 5th grade teacher, notices that some of his students are not doing as well as he would like in mathematics. At times, they don't even seem to be trying. With a unit on graphing coming up, Mr. Rodriguez sees an opportunity to focus on reinforcing effort. He announces to his students that as part of their graphing unit, they are going to use Microsoft Excel to graph their effort against quiz and homework scores for a two-week period. To help students rate their effort more precisely, he also distributes a rubric he found on Rubric Machine

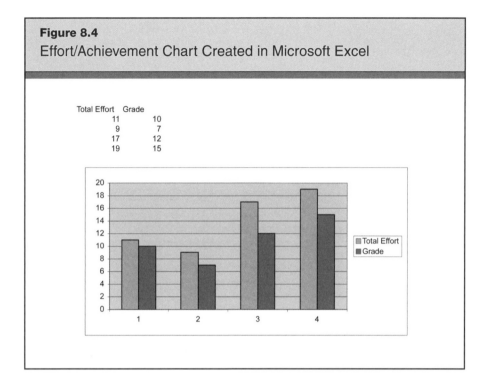

Figure 8.4
Effort/Achievement Chart Created in Microsoft Excel

(www.landmark-project.com/rubric_builder/index.php) by searching on the word "effort." As they track their effort and scores, Mr. Rodriguez's students begin to recognize that when they work harder and in specific ways, they earn better grades on their quizzes and homework checks, and do better overall in mathematics class. With his guidance, they begin to set objectives to improve in certain areas by increasing or refocusing their efforts. By paying attention to the learning expectations on the rubric, they see a relationship between effort and achievement.

Try using spreadsheet software to clarify this relationship with your students. Even very young students can, for example, keep track of how often they studied a family of mathematics facts and compare that frequency to how quickly and accurately they are able to recall the answers during a quiz (see Figure 8.5).

After analyzing this chart, Mr. Rodriguez's students might set an objective to put more effort into their studying for quizzes, as it obviously pays off in higher scores. In addition, Mr. Rodriguez could create a more detailed chart that shows student performance keyed to specific mathematics standards. For instance, if a student is doing

Figure 8.5
Chart Comparing Effort to Scores
Created in Microsoft Excel

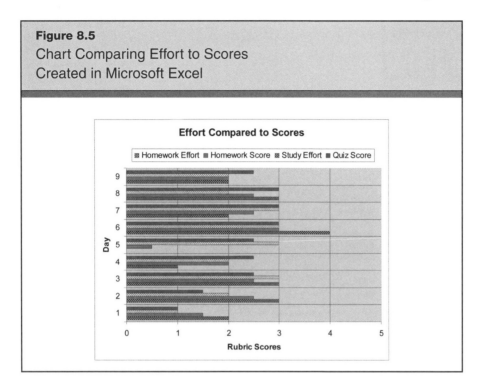

well in all areas except estimating, Mr. Rodriguez and the student might set an objective designed to improve the student's ability to estimate.

○ Data Collection Tools

A powerful way to convince students that effort is truly tied to achievement is to show them data—not just data on themselves, but also combined data on groups that they associate themselves with; for example, 5th grade students, social studies students, and incoming freshmen. When students see that others have faced many of the same difficulties they face and have overcome these obstacles and achieved goals with strong effort and good attitude, they too can see the connection between effort and achievement. In this way, teachers are following the classroom recommendation of explicitly teaching the importance of effort. When students have well-known or personal stories from which to learn, effort is reinforced, and students begin to take more responsibility for their own success.

Without the enhancement of technology, reinforcing effort in schools is often done through individual teacher comments or by collecting and sharing vignettes, testimonials, and observations from the learning community. For example, one elementary school uses a bulletin board near the main office. The title of the bulletin board is "Caught in the Act of Trying Hard," and on it are the collected stories of students putting forth a strong effort to achieve. Maintaining this bulletin board not only reinforces effort but also provides recognition (see Chapter 3).

Now let's look at how technology could enhance this initiative. The faculty and staff observational data, which were the basis for the bulletin board, could be collected online, through the school's Web site. The school might dedicate a section of its Web site to showing these examples: reinforcing effort and reassuring students that they too can succeed if they keep trying. Student success stories like these are more meaningful and more relatable than stories of larger-than-life heroes. This is particularly important for high school students who can grow more and more discouraged by their perceived failures, give up, and ultimately drop out of school.

You and others in your school might carry out more formal data collection with online surveys, such as those mentioned in the chapters focusing on setting objectives (Chapter 1) and providing feedback (Chapter 2). This technology allows you to use a standard effort rubric and incorporate it into a survey that will give you insight into the character of your students and provide data you can use to encourage students to try hard and to underscore the connection between effort and achievement.

Consider this example. Mr. Ekuban is charged with managing freshman orientation at his high school, and he wants to ensure that the new 9th graders appreciate the role that effort plays in achievement. Using an original rubric based on one he located on RubiStar (http://rubistar.4teachers.org), he designs a free survey with Survey Monkey (www.surveymonkey.com) to collect anonymous effort data and stories from the school's juniors and seniors in the National Honor Society. Mr. Ekuban then shares the survey data with the incoming freshmen to show them the ways in which students like them have overcome difficulties and achieved with strong effort and good attitude. An excerpt of his survey and some of the data it generated are shown in Figures 8.6 and 8.7.

Figure 8.6
Survey on Effort Created with Survey Monkey

High School Success — Effort & Attitude

1. Directions:

You have been chosen to provide insight to future high school students about what it takes to be successful in terms of effort and attitude. We would like to know how effort and attitude have affected your achievements.

Please read the following questions and indicate the degree in which they apply to you. Then in the last question, please give us a personal example of how you have managed to overcome a difficulty with effort and attitude. This difficulty should be related to your time in high school and not have had an immediately evident solution.

1. During my time in high school, I have been...

Unsuccessful	Sometimes successful	Mostly successful	Very successful
◡	◡	◡	◡

2. I actively seek out advice and support from family, neighbors, friends, or other adults in pursuit of my high school achievement goals.

Rarely	Sometimes	Usually	Very Often
◡	◡	◡	◡

3. I understand the boundaries of "work" and "play" and try to stay within those boundaries to be a responsible person.

Rarely	Sometimes	Usually	Very Often
◡	◡	◡	◡

4. I show my commitment to learning in and outside of school by putting forth my best efforts and persevering until objectives are accomplished.

Rarely	Sometimes	Usually	Very Often
◡	◡	◡	◡

5. I know that if I try hard enough, I can achieve my goals.

Strongly Disagree	Disagree	Agree	Strongly Agree
◡	◡	◡	◡

Reproduced courtesy of SurveyMonkey.com.

Figure 8.7
Survey Results from Survey Monkey

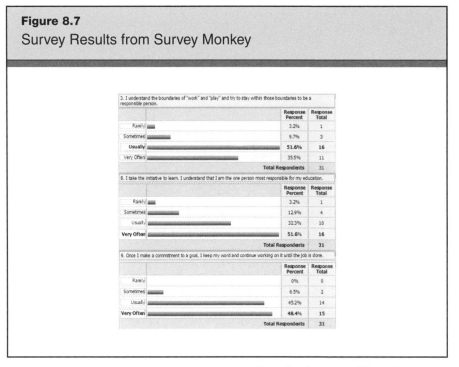

Reproduced courtesy of SurveyMonkey.com.

As you might suspect, these data also alerted Mr. Ekuban to common success factors unique to his school. This awareness helped him show his students the relationship between effort and achievement.

A survey like this is good for more than just collecting overall effort data. You might also use it with specific projects, such as science fairs, research papers, or other class projects, to show students what it takes to do that project well.

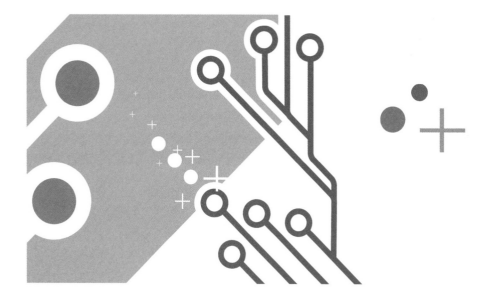

IV. Which Strategies Will Help Students Practice, Review, and Apply Learning?

After the classroom experience of acquiring and integrating new skills knowledge, students need time to practice, review, and apply this new learning so that they can make it permanent. During this phase of the learning process, students clear up any confusion and misconceptions they might have formed. They perfect their performance to eliminate errors. They also may apply their new skills by engaging in a project. Part IV focuses on the categories of strategies that help students to accomplish these tasks: *identifying similarities and differences* (Chapter 9); *homework and practice* (Chapter 10); and *generating and testing hypotheses* (Chapter 11).

9

IDENTIFYING SIMILARITIES AND DIFFERENCES

Asking students to *identify similarities and differences* in the content they are learning helps them restructure their understanding of that content. During the process, they make new connections, experience fresh insights, and correct misconceptions. These complex reasoning procedures lead students to deeper understanding.

McREL's research on identifying similarities and differences supports the following generalizations:

GENERALIZATIONS

1. Presenting students with explicit guidance in identifying similarities and differences enhances their understanding of and ability to use knowledge.
2. Asking students to independently identify similarities and differences enhances their understanding of and ability to use knowledge.
3. Representing similarities and differences in graphic or symbolic form enhances students' understanding of and ability to use knowledge.

4. Identification of similarities and differences can be accomplished in a variety of ways and is a highly robust activity.

Based these findings, we have five recommendations for classroom practice:

RECOMMENDATIONS

1. Teach students to use comparing, classifying, metaphors, and analogies when they identify similarities and differences.
2. Give students a model of the steps for engaging in the process.
3. Use a familiar context to teach students these steps.
4. Have students use graphic organizers as a visual tool to represent the similarities and differences.
5. Guide students as they engage in this process. Gradually give less structure and less guidance.

Technology facilitates the process of identifying similarities and differences by helping to create graphic organizers for comparing, classifying, creating metaphors, and creating analogies. In this chapter, we show how to use the following resources to help students identify similarities and differences: *word processing applications, spreadsheet applications, organizing and brainstorming software,* and *data collection tools.*

◔ Word Processing Applications

Graphic organizers are a time-tested way of representing similarities and differences, and we discuss them at length in the upcoming section on organizing and brainstorming software (see page 179). But what if you don't have Inspiration or Kidspiration? No problem. You can show your students how to use the Microsoft Word Drawing toolbar to draw diagrams, charts, or other templates to compare and classify items or illustrate metaphor or analogy. (And by doing so, you will be following two of the classroom recommendations for this strategy: having students use graphic organizers as a visual tool to represent the similarities and differences, and guiding students as they engage in this process.) AutoShapes provides a variety of lines, basic shapes, and connectors—everything you need to create the graphic organizers we describe. You can even find a Venn diagram in AutoShapes, or you can draw it by clicking Diagram under the Insert menu. You can make this graphic organizer more complex by adding additional overlapping circles to compare more categories than the traditional Venn diagram does. You can also select from several diagram types, changing your graphic organizer from a Venn diagram to a target, radial, cycle, or pyramid design. By enlarging the circles and using text boxes to add words to the diagram, you will be able to reflect the similarities and differences of any concept.

Creating classification tables and templates is possibly the best way to use a word processor to support identifying similarities and differences. Remember that classifying is the process of grouping things into definable categories on the basis of their attributes. Word processors make this easy. In the example shown in Figure 9.1, Ms. Fisher gives her students a list of geography terms. Students define the key categories they feel are best to group the items, then copy and paste the terms into the chart they create. The copy and paste features of any word processor allow students to classify terms again and again, based on new category definitions. Students can classify

Figure 9.1
Geography Classification Table Created in Microsoft Word

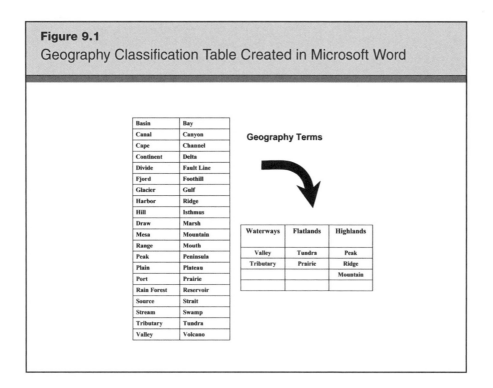

terms by elevation and then classify again based on geography terms that relate most strongly to water or land. Throughout the process, students view the terms in new ways.

Figure 9.2 shows a second example. Here, Mr. Andrews takes his literature students' work with classification to a more abstract level in order to build their understanding of different literary genres. He presents students with a list of titles they have read in class and the categories of Blue, Purple, Red, and Yellow, which, he explains, will represent four categories that the students will define for themselves. Then he begins the classification activity by asking students to suggest common themes among these books. They also brainstorm other classification possibilities, such as grouping the books by genre, time period, or another characteristic (e.g., short and long, easy and hard, male authors and female authors). Students then work individually to create their own categories and classify the books in the list by placing them in the appropriate category. Note that students engage in this activity after having read and studied the books, meaning they are identifying similarities and differences in a familiar context, which is in line with one of the classroom recommendations.

Figure 9.2
Book Classification Table Created in Microsoft Word

Blue	Purple	Red	Yellow
Hamlet	Huckleberry Finn	To Kill a Mockingbird	The Catcher in the Rye
A Tale of Two Cities	The Outsiders		Where the Red Fern Grows
	Gone with the Wind		

Define your categories and categorize the following books from the Junior-Senior reading list:

- Hamlet
- Where the Red Fern Grows
- Huckleberry Finn
- To Kill a Mockingbird
- The Catcher in the Rye
- A Tale of Two Cities
- The Outsiders
- The Grapes of Wrath
- Gone with the Wind
- Death of a Salesman
- Wuthering Heights

Throughout the activity, the students must return to their categories, reconsider them, and think about the books and categories in new ways. They also must think about their classification rationales and how they will defend their choices. The activity concludes with Mr. Andrews asking his students to exchange their completed charts and see if others can identify the classification criteria they're using. Try this yourself with the example in Figure 9.2. Can you figure it out? The student who created this example used Blue to indicate books with a theme of revenge; Purple to indicate books where the main characters deal with individual vs. society conflict; Red to indicate books dealing with race equality and relations; and Yellow to indicate books that contain "coming of age" themes.

So far, we've looked at some examples that engage students in sorting and classifying. Now let's look at how students might work on the related skill of recognizing and creating analogies, which require students to identify a similarity between two elements.

Mr. Purcell uses word processing software, a laptop, and a projector with his elementary class to create and display an "Analogy of the Day" thinking puzzle (see Figure 9.3).

Figure 9.3
Analogy of the Day Puzzle Created in Microsoft Word

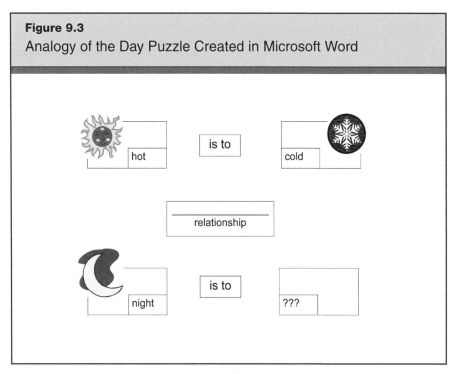

Clip art images © 2007 Jupiterimages Corporation.

He starts the year with teacher-created examples, primarily simple ones such as this:

Hot is to Cold as Night is to _____
Hard is to _____ as High is to Low.

As students get better at solving the analogy comparisons over a period of months, Mr. Purcell allows individual students to take over the Analogy of the Day activity and create a new puzzle for each day. (He does provide one-on-one help if it is needed.) Mr. Purcell also uses this opportunity to familiarize those students who don't have home access to technology with some easy operational tasks. Artistic students (and teachers too) can use the Drawing tools of a word processor to create illustrative graphics. The Internet is also a great resource for graphics to add to analogy puzzles. Those in Figure 9.3 were acquired from www.clipart.com. With this activity, Mr. Purcell is following the classroom recommendations of modeling this strategy for his students by guiding them through the process of creating analogies and gradually allowing them more and more independence applying the strategy on their own.

○ Spreadsheet Software

Spreadsheet software facilitates the comparison of data, making it an ideal tool to use with students to help them identify similarities and differences.

Spreadsheet templates can help teachers in the primary grades implement this strategy. For example, Ms. Li's 2nd graders are studying the planets of the Milky Way, including their sizes, masses, and gravitational pulls. To clarify the concept of gravitational pull, Ms. Li wants her students to grasp how their weight—a function of gravity— would vary on the planets in our solar system, including the dwarf planet, Pluto. She begins her planning by researching how to calculate one's weight on the various planets. (Two such resources that address this are www.factmonster.com/ipka/A0875450.html and www. teachervision.fen.com/astronomy/lesson-plan/353.html.) She finds that making these calculations is a matter of multiplying one's weight on Earth by the gravity of the other planet in relation to the Earth's gravity. If Earth's gravity is 1, the relative gravity of the other planets and the moon are as follows:

Earth:	1	The moon:	.17
Venus:	.9	Mars:	.38
Mercury:	.38	Jupiter:	2.38
Saturn:	.92	Uranus:	.89
Neptune:	1.13	Pluto:	.07

Because Ms. Li wants her 2nd graders to focus on the differences of the gravitational pulls rather than the mathematics of multiplying decimals, she creates a template in Excel that automatically calculates the child's weight on the planets when the child enters his or her weight. Figure 9.4 shows the spreadsheet template.

Let's take a closer look at how this template works. Ms. Li enters a formula for each cell from B2 through B11. She first clicks on cell B2, which is Mercury's row. Then in the formula bar, she types the formula =B1*.4, telling the software to multiply whatever value that is typed into B1 (the child's weight) by .4, and to place this product in cell B2. When she clicks in cell B3, she types the formula =B1*.9, telling the software to multiply the value in B1 by .9. She continues in this way until each cell from B2 through B11 has a formula for calculating the child's weight on that particular planet.

Now all the student has to do is enter his or her weight in cell B1, and the spreadsheet will automatically calculate the weight on the different planets. If Ms. Li has already created a chart using the Chart

Figure 9.4
Comparison Spreadsheet Template Created
in Microsoft Excel: My Weight on Different Planets

Enter your weight in pounds here:	0
Mercury	0
Venus	0
Earth	0
Moon	0
Mars	0
Jupiter	0
Saturn	0
Uranus	0
Neptune	0
Pluto (dwarf planet)	0

Wizard, the chart also will update automatically. Figures 9.5 and 9.6 show the spreadsheet with a child's weight of 50 pounds and the resulting chart.

Figure 9.5
Completed Comparison Spreadsheet:
My Weight on Different Planets

Enter your weight in pounds here:	**50**
Mercury	19
Venus	45
Earth	50
Moon	8.5
Mars	19
Jupiter	119
Saturn	46
Uranus	44.5
Neptune	56.5
Pluto (dwarf planet)	3.5

Figure 9.6
Comparison Chart Created in Microsoft Excel:
My Weight on Different Planets

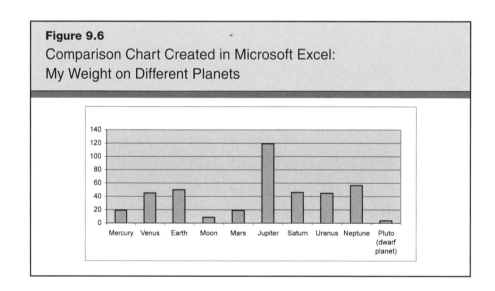

With the bar graph, students have a nonlinguistic representation of their weights on different planets. Ms. Li goes on to use these data to talk with her students about the similarities and differences in the planets' sizes, masses, and gravitational pulls. By comparing the differences, students begin to analyze the differences in planetary sizes and other characteristics that could affect their weight.

In another school, Mrs. Lokken, a 10th grade science teacher, uses Excel to show similarities and differences with older students. In her class, students have been collecting data on sunrise and sunset times for cities across the world from www.timeanddate.com. The learning goal is for students to see how a location's latitude affects the length of its days during various time spans throughout the year. After they collect selected cities' sunrise and sunset times for one month, the students work collaboratively in groups of three to enter the data into a spreadsheet. The next step is to subtract the sunrise time from the sunset time in order to find the length of each day, but before they can do that, they must first reformat the times into military time. To do this, they select cells B3 to G12 by clicking into B3 and dragging across the cells diagonally to G12. They then right-click (with a PC) or Control-click (with a Mac) and chose Format Cells. Here, they choose Custom and h:mm (to forgo an A.M. or P.M. display) then OK (see Figure 9.7.).

Figure 9.7

Comparison Chart Created in Microsoft Excel: Sunrise and Sunset Times in Various Cities

◇	A	B	C	D	E	F	G	H
1		Melbourne, Australia	Miami, FL, USA	Buenos Aires, Argentina	Juneau, AK, USA	Quito, Ecuador	Moscow, Russia	
2	Latitude	37° 52' S	25° 47' N	34° 20' S	58° 18' N	0° 14' S	55° 45' N	
3	Aug 2 sunrise	7:19	6:48	7:46	4:51	6:17	5:37	
4	Aug 2 sunset	17:33	20:08	18:14	21:15	18:23	21:34	
5	Aug 4 sunrise	7:17	6:49	7:45	4:55	6:17	5:40	
6	Aug 4 sunset	17:35	20:05	18:16	21:10	18:23	21:30	
7	Aug 11 sunrise	7:09	6:52	7:38	5:11	6:16	5:54	
8	Aug 11 sunset	17:41	20:00	18:21	20:53	18:22	21:14	
9	Aug 18 sunrise	7:00	6:55	7:30	5:26	6:15	6:07	
10	Aug 18 sunset	17:46	19:54	18:26	20:35	18:21	20:58	
11	Aug 30 sunrise	6:44	7:00	7:15	5:52	6:11	6:30	
12	Aug 30 sunset	17:57	19:42	18:34	20:02	18:18	20:28	
13								
14								
15								

Now they need to insert rows to create space to display the calculated lengths of each city's days. To do this, they click in the row beneath the sunset time for each day and Insert > Row. Next, they instruct Excel to subtract the sunrise time from the sunset time to find the length of the day. Mrs. Lokken provides these instructions:

1. Click into the blank cell beneath Melbourne's August 2 sunset time (in this case, cell B5).
2. In the formula bar above the graph, type in the formula =B4–B3. You are instructing Excel to find the difference between the values of B4 and B3 and to place the answer in the selected cell, B5. Then click Enter or Return.
3. The difference of 10 hours and 14 minutes (10:14) should appear in cell B5. This was the length of the day on August 2, 2005, in Melbourne, Australia.
4. Continue clicking into the appropriate cells and typing the formula in order to find the length of day for each city for each day listed. Alternatively, depending on your comfort level, you can apply the same formula across a row by clicking into a row that has a formula (B5) and dragging the + sign across the row.

By following Ms. Lokken's instructions, the students produce charts that look like the example in Figure 9.8.

Figure 9.8
Comparison Chart Stage 2:
Rows Inserted and Day Lengths Calculated

◇	A	B	C	D	E	F	G	H
1		Melbourne, Australia	Miami, FL, USA	Buenos Aires, Argentina	Juneau, AK, USA	Quito, Ecuador	Moscow, Russia	
2	Latitude	37° 52' S	25° 47' N	34° 20' S	58° 18' N	0° 14' S	55° 45' N	
3	Aug 2 sunrise	7:19	6:48	7:46	4:51	6:17	5:37	
4	Aug 2 sunset	17:33	20:06	18:14	21:15	18:23	21:34	
5	2-Aug	10:14	13:18	10:28	16:24	12:06	15:57	
6	Aug 4 sunrise	7:17	6:49	7:45	4:55	6:17	5:40	
7	Aug 4 sunset	17:35	20:05	18:16	21:10	18:23	21:30	
8	4-Aug	10:18	13:16	10:31	16:15	12:06	15:50	
9	Aug 11 sunrise	7:09	6:52	7:38	5:11	6:16	5:54	
10	Aug 11 sunset	17:41	20:00	18:21	20:53	18:22	21:14	
11	11-Aug	10:32	13:08	10:43	15:42	12:06	15:20	
12	Aug 18 sunrise	7:00	6:55	7:30	5:26	6:15	6:07	
13	Aug 18 sunset	17:46	19:54	18:26	20:35	18:21	20:58	
14	18-Aug	10:46	12:59	10:56	15:09	12:06	14:51	
15	Aug 30 sunrise	6:44	7:00	7:15	5:52	6:11	6:30	
16	Aug 30 sunset	17:57	19:42	18:34	20:02	18:18	20:28	
17	30-Aug	11:13	12:42	11:19	14:10	12:07	13:58	
18								

The instructions continue:

5. In the blank cells in Column A, label the cells with the date. For example, in cell A5, type "August 2". Excel will automatically reformat the date based upon the default settings.

6. Because you no longer need the sunrise and sunset times, you can hide those cells. To do this, select a row to hide, such as Row 3, and click on Window and Hide, or right-click (Control-click on a Mac) and choose Hide. A row can be unhidden by clicking on the bold line that represents the hidden row and dragging down or by right-clicking between the two rows (Control-click on a Mac) and choosing Unhide.

At this point, the graphs look like the one in Figure 9.9.

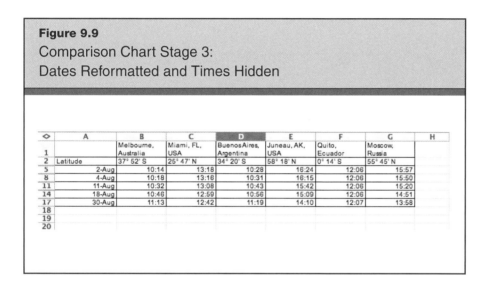

Figure 9.9

Comparison Chart Stage 3:

Dates Reformatted and Times Hidden

◇	A	B	C	D	E	F	G	H
1		Melbourne, Australia	Miami, FL, USA	Buenos Aires, Argentina	Juneau, AK, USA	Quito, Ecuador	Moscow, Russia	
2	Latitude	37° 52' S	25° 47' N	34° 20' S	58° 18' N	0° 14' S	55° 45' N	
5	2-Aug	10:14	13:18	10:28	16:24	12:06	15:57	
8	4-Aug	10:18	13:16	10:31	16:15	12:06	15:50	
11	11-Aug	10:32	13:08	10:43	15:42	12:06	15:20	
14	18-Aug	10:46	12:59	10:56	15:09	12:06	14:51	
17	30-Aug	11:13	12:42	11:19	14:10	12:07	13:58	
18								
19								
20								

Back to the instructions:

7. You also can hide the Latitude row or Cut and Paste it below the rest of the information, as it will not be included in the graph.
8. Select the data to graph, that is, the names of the cities, the dates, and the length of days for each date. You can select multiple rows by holding down the Control button.
9. Click on the Chart Wizard icon. It looks like a red, yellow, and blue bar chart.
10. The Chart Wizard will ask you to choose a chart type. Think about which charts work best with which types of data. A pie chart, for example, is not useful for this type of data. Experiment with a few charts to see which works best. For this lesson, we will make a scatter plot, so select Scatter.
11. Experiment with Rows and Columns to determine the best way to depict the trends. In this demonstration, the user chooses Columns.
12. Label your graph "Length of Day." Label the X and Y axes, if desired.
13. You now have the option of showing a small version of the chart on the same page as the data or on its own page as a larger picture. Click Finish when you are done.

The finished charts look similar to the example in Figure 9.10.

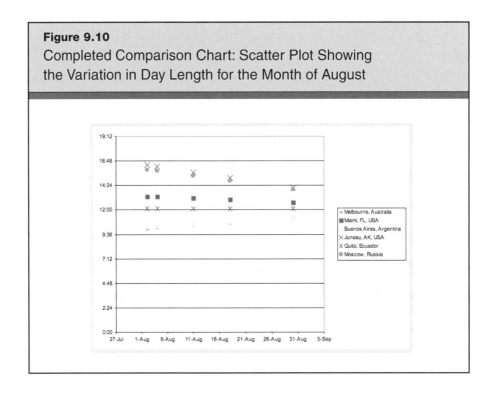

Figure 9.10

Completed Comparison Chart: Scatter Plot Showing the Variation in Day Length for the Month of August

With the charts set up, Mrs. Lokken and her students can use them as tools for content analysis. Here are some questions she asks:

- What predictions can you make about how the graph will look in December?
- Why is Quito's length of day unaffected by the change in seasons?
- Why do you think Miami shows only a small change?
- What are some reasons why the icons representing Buenos Aires and Melbourne are nearly superimposed?
- Is there a date when all cities will generally be on the same line? If so, on which line? On which date? When will this reoccur?

In this example, note the extent to which technology facilitates the processes of analyzing the similarities and differences, explaining the trends found, and predicting future patterns. Consider how difficult and impractical this activity would have been without technology.

○ Organizing and Brainstorming Software

Kidspiration (for grades preK–5) and Inspiration (for intermediate and older students) are great tools to help you scaffold learning experiences for your students. By first ensuring that students are comfortable using graphic organizer models and templates in pairs, groups, or individually, you can more easily progress to student-created graphic organizers. Use of graphic organizers helps students visually portray connections and experience new and deeper insights about the content.

One of the simplest but most effective ways to help students compare two or more items is to use the Venn diagram template located in the Thinking Skills folder of Inspiration templates and in the More Activities folder of Kidspiration templates. Figure 9.11 shows one of the Venn diagrams Mrs. Craig helps her 3rd graders create during a lesson focused on broadening and expanding their knowledge of the similarities and differences between the United States and England. After comparing traditional foods, they compare holidays, and then historical events of both countries. Next, the students go on to create individual diagrams to compare another category they find personally interesting.

Another template similar to a Venn diagram is Inspiration's Comparison template, used in Figure 9.12 and found in the Thinking Skills folder. You should also look at the Book Comparison template in the

Figure 9.11
Venn Diagram Created in Inspiration

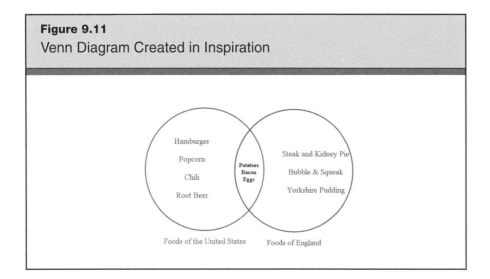

Language Arts folder. Book Comparison allows students to track and visualize information about literary works, including similarities and differences in authors' lives and styles and in the works' themes, tone, mood, and messages to the reader. Figure 9.12 shows how Mr. Young's high school students use this template to compare the epic poem *Beowulf* with John Gardner's novel *Grendel*.

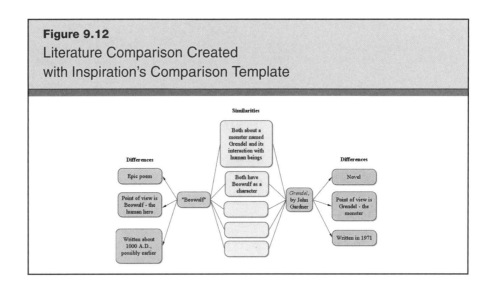

Figure 9.12

Literature Comparison Created
with Inspiration's Comparison Template

Younger students with minimal writing skills or students who best remember facts presented through nonlinguistic representation (see Chapter 3) also benefit from organizing and brainstorming software. Kidspiration and Inspiration include hundreds of graphics and symbols for students to use. If the desired graphic is not part of an existing symbol library, students can use the Symbol Maker tool in Kidspiration or create a custom symbol library using graphics from the Internet or photos taken with a digital camera. Students of all ages can also use their voices to record thoughts and ideas about similarities and differences. Figure 9.13 shows a comparison that a 2nd grader created with Kidspiration's Comparison template, found in the More Activities folder.

Just as organizing and brainstorming software facilitates comparison, it also works for classification. Several classification templates are available, and custom templates are easy to create. Figure 9.14 shows the Animal Classification template, found in Kidspiration's

Science folder. Students can search through the software's graphics library to find the animals that fit in each classification category.

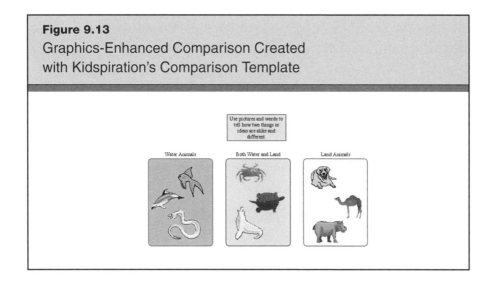

Figure 9.13
Graphics-Enhanced Comparison Created with Kidspiration's Comparison Template

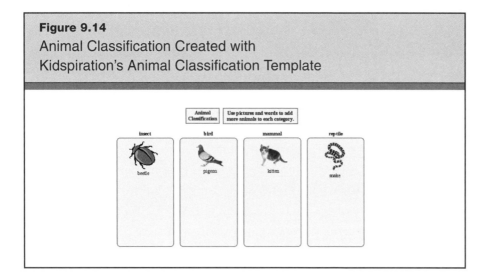

Figure 9.14
Animal Classification Created with Kidspiration's Animal Classification Template

Teachers can expand this activity by asking students to use the writing feature of Kidspiration and Inspiration to brainstorm how these animals are alike and different. The more similarities and differences students can describe, the stronger their knowledge of animals becomes.

One final example, seen in Figure 9.15, shows a more advanced use of Kidspiration featuring the Classifying Ideas template found in the More Activities folder. In science class, Mrs. Nelson gives her 3rd grade students a list of words and asks them to use the three titles for their categories and sort the words. For each word, the students key in an explanation of why the word belongs in that particular category.

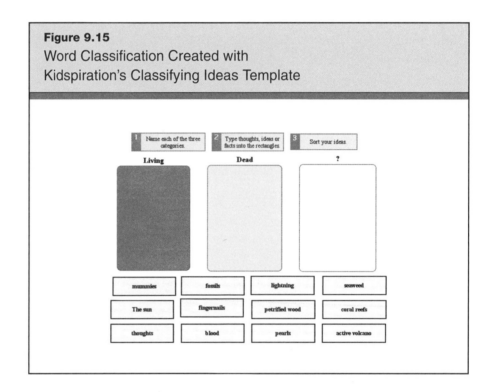

Figure 9.15
Word Classification Created with
Kidspiration's Classifying Ideas Template

○ Data Collection Tools

Comparing and classifying usually requires data. Many tools are available to help students define characteristics in order to identify similarities and differences. Let's look at how an elementary teacher might combine this instructional strategy with the strategy of nonlinguistic representation (see Chapter 5) during a science lesson on density by using data collection tools to measure the mass and volume of various objects.

Mrs. Wesolowski wants to teach her 5th grade class the concept of density as a characteristic of materials. Her goals are to make sure all her students understand that density is how much mass is packed into a certain volume, and to dispel common misconceptions about the relationship between volume and mass. For instance, most students think that larger objects are always more massive and vice versa. They also tend to think that materials have all of the same characteristics or all different characteristics. Mrs. Wesolowski's goal is to have her students understand the possible combinations of similarities and differences in material characteristics.

She decides to guide her students through a set of three density experiments by independently varying volume, mass, and density. To measure mass, they'll be using a digital scale instead of a traditional balance. The objects students need to measure all have small masses, and the fine accuracy the digital scale provides allows them to capture minute but significant differences in mass for their calculations. The students are also able to connect the digital scale to a computer by USB cable to take multiple measurements.

Mrs. Wesolowski gives her students a spreadsheet template to multiply length by width by height to calculate volume and then divide mass by volume to get the density in grams per cubic centimeter (g/cm^3). After leading her class through a science inquiry planning process, including making some predictions, she guides her students through three experiments:

1. Students collect and calculate volume, mass, and density data on a rectangular sponge. Then they soak the same sponge in melted wax and let the wax harden. Students again collect the data and calculate density. By keeping the volume the same but changing the mass (with the wax), they are able to see that density is dependent on the concentration of mass.

2. Students use scissors to trim a rectangular sponge until its mass equals that of a $1cm^3$ density cube on the digital scale. (These cubes are available from science education supply retailers.) Once the masses are equalized, students again collect data and calculate the density of both objects. By keeping the mass the same but varying the volume, students can see that density also is dependent on volume.

3. Now that the students have used data collection to calculate density and compare objects, they see that density is related to both mass and volume independently. In a third experiment, they combine the first two experiments. Using red and blue Lego building blocks

that are identical in shape and size, they construct one all-red cube and one all-blue cube, making the blue cube larger than the red one. Again the students collect volume and mass data, and then calculate volume with the spreadsheet. Some students are surprised to find that the densities of the two cubes are the same. Then they realize that density is a characteristic of the material (plastic). Even if the both the mass and volume are different, the ratio of mass to volume is the same. The different colors of the cubes underscore the idea that objects can look different in many ways but still have the same density.

As you can see, in this lesson, technology is the key to accurate comparisons. It also facilitates quick computations so the students can focus on the density concepts. Now let's look at an example of how observational data collection facilitates identifying similarities and differences through classification.

Mr. Brewer gives his 4th grade students a matrix for classifying "bugs." He doesn't tell them about the various categories they might use, such as insect (e.g., beetles), arachnid (e.g., spiders), and myria-pod (e.g., centipedes); he will introduce these categories later, after the students have had a chance to think critically about the characteristics that will help them identify similarities and differences necessary to classify bug specimens.

With this organizer distributed, Mr. Brewer now provides the students with an assorted collection of bug specimens encased in plastic, which he found at his science education supply retailer. Using a ProScope, his students view magnified images of the specimens and use the matrix to classify them. At first, students categorize by all sorts of traits, such as color, size, and eye shape. Eventually, with some guidance from Mr. Brewer, students see that number of legs, antennae, and body segments are important defining characteristics. Some students also subcategorize the specimens by the presence of wings, fangs, and both wings and fangs. As Figure 9.16 shows, these students rearrange their matrix into three categories, using the observational data (magnified pictures) and the actual category names.

To combine this activity with the strategy of homework and practice (see Chapter 10), Mr. Brewer has his students visit www.museum. vic.gov.au/bugs/catcher/index.aspx to take advantage of the huge bug collection of the Museum Victoria in Australia. The Web site allows his students to conduct similar activities by playing an interactive game called *Bug Catcher.*

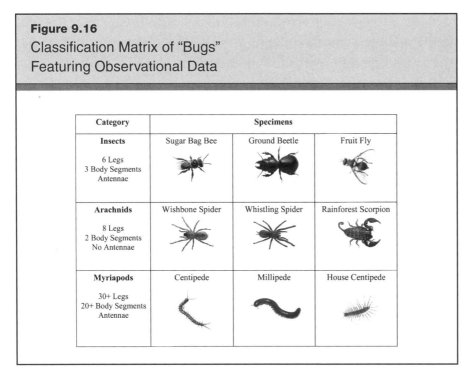

Figure 9.16

Classification Matrix of "Bugs" Featuring Observational Data

Photographs by Alan Henderson. Reproduced courtesy of Museum Victoria.

Data collection probeware is also very useful for identifying similarities and differences because its computer interface allows students to quickly create all sorts of graphical representations for comparison. An example of this is an experiment led by Mr. McGuire. After teaching his Algebra I class to calculate and graph the slope of a line, he uses a motion detector probe connected to a computer to help the students apply their knowledge, using the feedback from the computer graphing program tied to the motion detector.

The students are required to try and match their movements with graphical representations of position versus time. As they move, a line plots in real time, overlaying the plot they are trying to match. After some practice, they are to identify the similarities and differences in their movements compared to the graphical plot. This shows them how motion can be represented graphically in a very realistic and fun way.

Figure 9.17 shows how one of Mr. McGuire's students needs to move to match the graphical plot. To get the graph to go up, he or she needs to move toward the detector and vice versa. Mr. McGuire also uses the strategy of generating and testing hypotheses (see Chapter 11) by having students practice with the detector and then predict what the plot will be if they move a certain way.

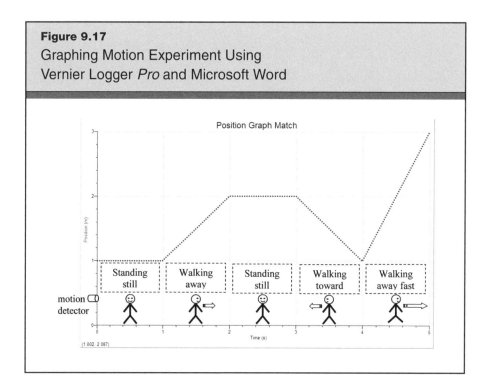

Figure 9.17

Graphing Motion Experiment Using
Vernier Logger *Pro* and Microsoft Word

10

HOMEWORK AND PRACTICE

H*omework* and *practice* give students a chance to review and apply what they have learned.

As an extension of the classroom, homework provides opportunities for students to deepen their understanding of the content and to gain proficiency with their skills. Despite these benefits, homework is not without controversy. The practices recommended in this section can help teachers and students get the most out of homework and avoid some of the pitfalls.

McREL's research on homework supports the following generalizations:

GENERALIZATIONS

1. The amount of homework assigned to students should be different from elementary to high school.
2. Parental involvement in doing homework should be kept to a minimum.
3. The purpose of homework should be identified and articulated.
4. If homework is assigned, it should be commented upon.

Based on these findings, we have three recommendations for classroom practice:

RECOMMENDATIONS

1. Establish and communicate a homework policy.
2. Design homework assignments that clearly articulate purpose and outcome.
3. Vary approaches to providing feedback.

Having students practice a skill or concept enhances their ability to reach the expected level of proficiency. Multiple exposures to material help students deepen their understanding of content and become proficient with skills. Typically, students need about 24 practice sessions with a skill in order to achieve 80-percent competency (Marzano et al., 2001, p. 67). Because it is easy for errors to slip in when students are practicing, teachers should give feedback as quickly as possible—ideally, early in the practice sessions, before students internalize erroneous processes and knowledge.

McREL's research on practice supports the following generalizations:

GENERALIZATIONS

1. Mastering a skill or process requires a fair amount of focused practice.
2. While practicing, students should adapt and shape what they have learned.

Based on these findings, we have three recommendations for the classroom:

RECOMMENDATIONS

1. Ask students to chart their speed and accuracy.
2. Design practice assignments that focus on specific elements of a complex skill or process.
3. Plan time for students to increase their conceptual understanding of skills or processes.

Technology facilitates homework and practice by providing a wealth of resources for learning outside of the classroom, making it easy for students to work on collaborative homework assignments and providing "drill and practice" resources that help students refine their skills.

In this chapter, we look at the categories of technology that enrich a classroom's homework program: *word processing applications, spreadsheet applications, multimedia, Web resources,* and *communication software.*

Word Processing Applications

Most people think of word processing software as a one-trick pony: You use it to type papers and that is it. However, the varied tools in word processing applications make it much more than an electronic typewriter.

In other sections of this book, we discuss many of the tools available in Microsoft Word, which is one of the most common word processing software products. One of the tools in Word that we haven't yet touched on is its research capability. Almost every teacher knows to send student researchers to search engines like Google or Yahoo!, but far fewer know that students can also search within Word. Clicking on Tools > Research brings up a research window on the right side of a Word document. From this window, students can search the Encarta dictionary, a thesaurus, the Encarta Encyclopedia, eLibrary, and more.

One real advantage to using this tool rather than opening a browser program and using a search engine is that the search results tend to be more focused than those generated by a general-purpose search engine. For younger students and other fledging researchers, this can be a significant benefit. Students who search from within a Word document are less likely to be sent on "wild goose chases" or to be diverted from the assignment by the Web's many distractions.

Here's an illustration of how students might use Word for research. Ms. Thompson is teaching her 5th graders about the Holocaust. For the unit's final project, she offers students a choice of topics, some of which are student-generated, and a choice of formats: a PowerPoint presentation, an iMovie, or a standard report.

Emma decides to do a report, as she has already created a PowerPoint and an iMovie for previous units. As she works on her report on her home computer, she comes across the word *persecution* in a text she's reading. Although Emma knows she has heard this word before, she isn't certain of its meaning, so she accesses the Word research tool from her open document and looks it up. The definition provided helps a little, but she still isn't sure that she completely gets the word's meaning. So Emma clicks on the thesaurus link in the research tool and reads some of the synonyms for persecution: *bullying, harassment,* and *discrimination.* The combination of the definition and the synonyms gives Emma a good idea of what the word means.

After she finishes the first draft of her report, Emma checks the grade level of her writing, as Ms. Thompson has taught her to do, using the Word spelling and grammar tool (see Chapter 2, page 43). She sees that her Flesch-Kincaid grade-level rating is only 4.9. Emma knows that she can increase the sophistication of her writing by using some of the new vocabulary words the class has been learning, changing some of the adjectives to more descriptive ones that she recognized in the Word thesaurus, and combining some of the short sentences she has a tendency to use. As a final check of her report, she uses the AutoSummarize tool (see Chapter 6, page 123) to see if the computer gives her a summary that really says what she is trying to express.

○ Spreadsheet Software

Whether it's on a home computer, classroom laptop, or school lab computer, using spreadsheets for homework and practice is typically about students using data to master concepts and skills. Students can practice by calculating, manipulating, and displaying data to gain deeper understanding.

Here's an example. Ryan Turnage teaches physical education and is a football coach at Caroline High School. His colleague, Mrs. Baker, teaches algebra. Mrs. Baker asks Coach Turnage to help motivate some of the players to practice their data analysis skills. Because he is in charge of the football team's strength and conditioning program, he decides to have his players track their workouts: how much weight they are lifting and the number of repetitions they are doing at each session. A computer lab is located just across from the locker room, so after each workout, he has his players open a spreadsheet to enter their data. Coach Turnage also has them correlate the data with their heart rate, which he has them take in the computer lab as they wait for the computers to boot up. Finally, the players save their spreadsheets to a central server folder for later use. At the end of the season, the players and coaches can check the progress of each player's workouts, and the players graph these data in Mrs. Baker's algebra class.

After the students become comfortable using spreadsheet software, Mrs. Baker has them use spreadsheets to deepen their understanding of parabolic functions. As part of her unit on graphing quadratic equations, she gives her students standard homework assignments focused on solving parabolic functions and hand-graphing. Next she brings technology back into the mix, instructing students to enter the answers to their homework problems into spreadsheets. They enter the x-value and the parabolic function into an Excel spreadsheet, allowing the program to calculate the y-values. Then they create an XY scatter plot with a smooth trend line to display the parabolic graph. Finally, the students practice making different plots by changing constant values. In order for the graphs to be comparable, only one constant is changed at a time, and the scale of the graphs is held constant. Her Excel spreadsheet instructions follow:

1. Enter x-values from -4 to $+4$. Enter the function in the adjoining cell to direct it to fill in the y-value. For example, if the first x-value is in cell A2, the function $y = 8x^2 + 4x + 5$ would be entered in cell B2 like this: =8*(A2^2)+4*A2+5. In other words, you are telling Excel to take the value that you type into cell A2, increase it by a power of two, and multiply by eight. Then you are telling Excel to multiply the value typed in A2 by four. Finally, Excel will add those two quantities to 5 and put the answer in cell B2.
2. Fill in the rest of the cells in column B to calculate the rest of the y-values. Use the function you placed in B2 by pasting it into the other B cells. Excel will change the formulas automatically by replacing the x-value with the A-column values A3, A4, A5, and so on, in the formula.
3. Highlight the data and choose Insert > Chart and select XY (Scatter).
4. Select Scatter with data points connected by smooth lines.

The students quickly make many parabolic graphs by changing one constant value at a time. (Figure 10.1 shows a few.) This would have taken much longer if students had to hand-graph all of the variations. With the aid of technology, the students are able to see many transformations of the parabolic plot. This leads to a discussion on how these shapes can be applied in real-life situations, such as in architectural design.

Figure 10.1
Parabolic Graphing Practice Activities
Created in Microsoft Excel

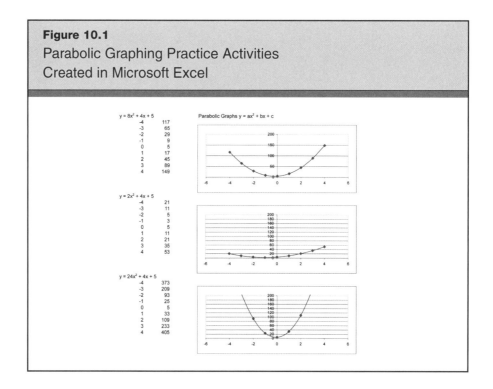

○ Multimedia

Clearly, using and creating multimedia requires a high degree of technology accessibility. Some schools check out computers and equipment to students, while others schools enjoy the benefits of one-to-one laptop programs in which students have a laptop assigned to them for the whole year. If they do not have a family computer to use, they can use their school laptop. When access is not a problem, multimedia homework is an opportunity to deepen understanding and gain proficiency. Practicing with multimedia allows students to shape the experience to their individual learning style and increase their level of understanding to mastery.

Well-made software allows teachers to choose which learning objectives the student needs to practice, has sophisticated and seamless multimedia to keep the learner engaged, and provides immediate feedback and scaffolding in order to help the student understand and practice the concept. New software titles emerge so often that instead of listing specific ones here, we have listed regularly updated resources that recognize the best educational software.

- EDDIE Awards
www.computedgazette.com/page3.html

Sponsored by ComputED, the Education Software Review Award("the EDDIEs") recognizes innovating software for education. Categories include Early Learning, Early Elementary, Upper Elementary, Middle School, High School/Post-Secondary, Internet Tools, Educational Websites, and Teacher Productivity Tools.

- BESSIE Awards
www.computedgazette.com/page11.html

Similar to the EDDIEs, the BESSIEs recognize the Best Educational Software. Categories include Early Elementary and Upper Elementary. These awards are sponsored by ComputED.

- *Technology & Learning*'s Awards of Excellence/Readers' Choice Awards
www.techlearning.com

In every December issue, the magazine *Technology & Learning* identifies the best software and hardware in the categories of Curriculum and Data Management; Language Arts; Math/Science; Multidisciplinary; Presentation/Productivity; Social Sciences and Life Skills; Teacher Resources/Professional Development; Tools for Communication; Collaboration, and System Management; Curriculum Software; and Educator Tools. In addition, *T&L* recognizes "tried and true" software used by professionals.

- eSchoolNews Readers' Choice Awards
www.eschoolnews.com/resources/surveys/editorial/rca/

This award is decided upon by nominations from readers of eSchoolNews. Categories include Multimedia Creation Tools, Math Software, Projectors and Interactive Whiteboards, School Science Software, and School Reading Software, among many others.

• CodIE Awards
www.siia.net/codies

This annual award, sponsored by the Software & Information Industry Association, recognizes software in various industries, education included. One of the categories is "Education Newcomer Award," for which users can nominate new outstanding educational software.

• Discovery Education's The Parent Channel
http://school.discovery.com/parents/reviewcorner/software/

Discovery Education compiles its educational software review by testing software with children and parents. The products selected for the list are well designed and encourage students as they learn. Each review provides a detailed synopsis of appropriate age, content, and caveats.

In addition to learning *from* multimedia such as educational games and interactive simulations, students can learn *with* multimedia by creating their own projects at home or at school to develop their understanding and practice skills.

When students create multimedia projects like those discussed in Chapter 5, they undertake many of the project's tasks outside of class. After planning their scripts and storyboards, students can search their homes and neighborhoods for imagery to incorporate via video. This creates more opportunities for creativity than the typical classroom and school offer.

Another example of creating multimedia for homework and practice is teacher or student construction of PowerPoint games. Students create a game using hyperlinks and action buttons in PowerPoint. Like any multimedia project, the game needs to be well planned before the actual PowerPoint design begins. Sarah Grabowski Lodick created such a PowerPoint game while completing her student teaching for the University of Georgia. She wanted her mathematics students to learn basic graphing skills using the Cartesian coordinate system, so she created a game called BattleGraph (see Figure 10.2), based on the Battleship board game, in which students customize the game or play it directly. The game uses x- and y-coordinates to place ships on a graphical ocean. A player also uses x- and y-coordinates to try to locate and hit the opposing player's ships.

Even students without home access to computers can play the game as it can be printed out in hard copy form. BattleGraph is available online at http://sarah.lodick.com/edit/powerpoint_game/battlegraph/battlegraph.ppt.

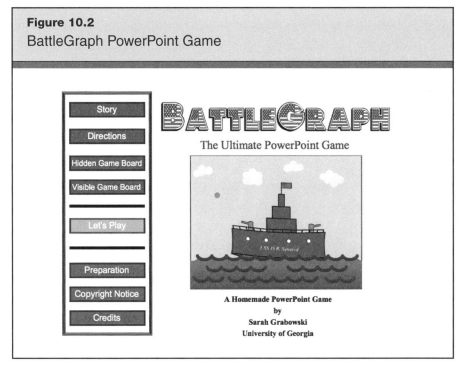

Figure 10.2
BattleGraph PowerPoint Game

Reproduced courtesy of Sarah Grabowski Lodick, MEd.

◯ Web Resources

Web resources allow students to practice concepts and skills repeatedly from their homes, during a study period, or even as an anchor activity in a differentiated classroom. Online educational games have an inherent appeal and generate immediate feedback that allows a student, parent, and teacher to monitor progress toward mastery. Online games help teachers meet the classroom recommendations of varying methods of providing feedback, helping students to focus on particular skills. The games also provide an incentive for students to chart their speed and accuracy, another of the recommendations.

Consider this example. Mrs. Metz's 3rd grade class is learning about acids, bases, and the pH scale. Although the students do several related experiments and activities at school, Mrs. Metz wants to ensure that they will remember the material when the unit is complete. Several weeks after the close of the unit, she asks them to go through the tutorial and activities on the Kitchen Chemistry PBS Zoom Web site (see the description of this resource on page 198).

At the end of the tutorial is a section to print out a reward certificate. To confirm that her students completed the activities, Mrs. Metz asks them to either print the reward certificate and hand it in, or save the certificate as a screen shot and e-mail it to her. Later, she will use a BrainPOP quiz to test for retention.

In another example, a 1st grade class is working on short vowel sounds, but some students are ready for more challenging work. One of their teacher's favorite resources for building reading skills is the Starfall Web site: www.starfall.com, which is a great resource for providing focused practice time on a particular skill—one of the classroom recommendations. During this particular class session, all Mrs. Metz's students go to the Learn to Read section of the Web site. Some do the short-vowel activities while others concentrate on long vowels and consonant blends. Each vowel sound links to a corresponding e-book where students can click on unfamiliar words and hear them "spoken." Students can also play a game designed to help build their knowledge of specific vowel sounds. The variety of activities and flexible presentation style means each student is able to work on skills that best meet his or her needs, and the teacher is able to differentiate instruction during practice sessions.

Here are some other recommended Web sites to use for homework and practice:

• BBC Skillswise
www.bbc.co.uk/skillswise

This resource from the BBC includes a Numbers section and a Words section. Within these sections are concept areas containing skill-sharpening worksheets, games, and quizzes appropriate for grades 3–8. Among the concepts covered are punctuation, fractions, suffixes, and multiplication.

• National Library of Virtual Manipulatives
http://nlvm.usu.edu/en/nav/vlibrary.html

This resource from Utah State University contains many virtual manipulatives to help students in grades preK–12 better understand mathematics concepts. Some of the manipulatives include base blocks, geoboards, algebra tiles, algebra balance scales, and various puzzles.

- ExploreLearning
www.explorelearning.com

ExploreLearning contains gizmos—virtual learning apparatuses—for secondary-level mathematics and science concepts. Among the gizmos available are ones that address how tides work, the multiplication of mixed numbers, and photosynthesis. Although ExploreLearning is a subscription-based site, a free five-minute trial period allows a site visitor to explore the resource. Each gizmo is followed by assessment questions to check for understanding.

- BrainPOP
http://www.brainpop.com

BrainPOP contains hundreds of short, Flash-based movies on nearly every curricular area: English, social studies, mathematics, science, health, and technology. Each movie is followed by a 10-question quiz that can be printed out or e-mailed to a teacher. This is a subscription-based site, but many movies are available for free.

- IKnowthat.com
www.iknowthat.com

This resource contains skill-building games for students in elementary and middle school. Some skills addressed include using correct punctuation, building speed with mathematics facts, and labeling maps of continents and the United States.

- Wizards & Pigs
www.cogcon.org/gamegoo/games/wiznpigs/wiznpigs.html

This is a game designed to help young students practice identifying alliteration, rhyming, and free verse.

- Flashcard Exchange
www.flashcardexchange.com

This resource allows teachers and students to generate custom virtual flashcards and access flashcards others have created. Teachers can create study guides for students or allow students to create their own. Students can play "memory" with the card stack, and they can also play a game designed to help build their knowledge of vowel sounds.

- Mousercise
www.3street.org/mouse

This resource helps students to learn and practice mouse control. Included are activities to introduce pull-down menus, radio buttons, scroll bars, checkboxes, and copying/pasting.

- Lever Tutorial
www.elizrosshubbell.com/levertutorial

This tutorial takes students through the parts of the lever and the three types of levers. Each minilesson is followed by a brief quiz.

- Kitchen Chemistry
http://pbskids.org/zoom/games/kitchenchemistry/virtual-start.html

This activity teaches students basic facts about acids and bases, then allows them to conduct virtual experiments by "mixing" substances to test for acidity and carbonation.

- Hurricane Strike!
http://meted.ucar.edu/hurrican/strike/index.htm

This simulation from the University Corporation for Atmospheric Research in Boulder, Colorado, takes students through tutorials about hurricanes and helps them apply what they've learned to make decisions as a hurricane approaches.

- Stellarium
www.stellarium.org

This free planetarium for your PC allows students to see the night sky from any location at any date specified. Students can watch constellations move across the sky in fast speed to get an idea of how the night sky changes with the seasons. Students can also "zoom" to planets and other celestial bodies.

- Instant Projects
http://instantprojects.org

This resource includes a template to help teachers easily create class Web sites. Teachers can post homework assignments that are accessible at any time.

○ Communication Software

Chapter 2's discussion of providing feedback covered how to use the Microsoft Word Track Changes and Insert Comments features to give feedback on student writing. Although these tools are an ideal way to let a few authors edit a piece of writing for peer review, there can be complicating factors. To edit a document collaboratively, all students must either have access to a shared folder (which may not be possible away from school) or must e-mail the document to other group members. Editing a document via e-mail can be confusing and cumbersome with a large group—often resulting in one version overwriting another or multiple versions of one document. In these circumstances, another option is to select communication software designed to facilitate collaboration.

Here's an example. A group of students in a high school family/consumer sciences class agree to perfect their recipe for Steak au Poivre as a final project. First, they will practice making the dish individually at home, and then they will compare recipes and results. What they need is a way to share their recipe adjustments. They decide to use Writeboard (http://writeboard.com), one of several services that allow multiple users to edit a document via the Web in a manner similar to a wiki. Users can compare different versions of their page and see changes made, much like the format of Track Changes in Word. As you can see in Figure 10.3, highlighted text and gray strikethroughs indicate the changes between the fourth and sixth versions of the students' recipe.

The Writeboard service can be combined with other free services offered by the company 37signals, such as Backpack Checklist and Campfire Chatroom. Backpack (www.backpackit.com) allows students to make individual or shared pages to organize notes, Web sites, to-do lists, and more. There is even a calendar feature to help with project planning. Campfire (www.campfirenow.com) is an online group chat tool. It allows students to collaborate between classrooms, schools, or even countries. Campfire chatrooms are password-protected so that students can instant-message safely.

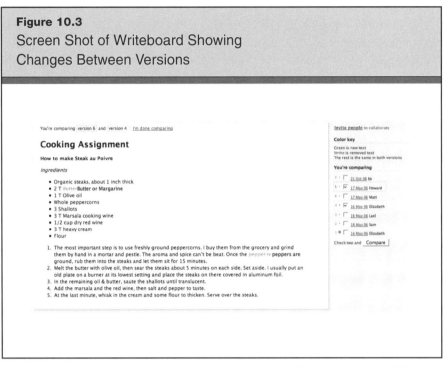

Reproduced courtesy of 37signals.

As the group gets closer to their final exam, they decide to use Backpack to organize their to-do list so that everyone can easily access their upcoming responsibilities (see Figure 10.4).

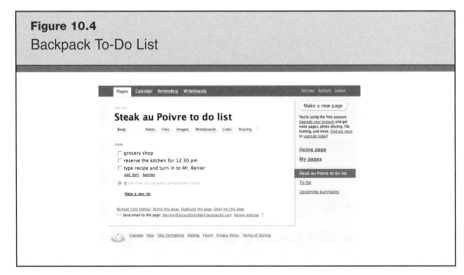

Reproduced courtesy of 37signals.

Note that one step—asking a fellow student's grandmother if they can use her china on the day of the final—has already been completed and checked off.

As these examples illustrate, using communication software facilitates the organization of group homework. This type of user editing and sharing on the Web is so different from the previously "read-only" Web that educational technologists often refer to these tools as "Web 2.0." Here are some other Web resources that offer similar services:

- Google Docs
http://docs.google.com

Google Docs works much like Writeboard but has a Microsoft Word–like interface that will be familiar to users.

- YourDraft
www.yourdraft.com

YourDraft has a very simple interface, sometimes referred to as "WYSIWYG" (pronounced "wizee wig"), which stands for "What You See Is What You Get." Windows Microsoft Word users will instantly recognize the interface. You can insert a picture or even a Flash component. There is no sign-in; you are simply given two versions of a Web address that contains your document. The first is a read-only version, and the second can be edited by you or anyone with whom you share the URL. Currently, YourDraft does not include a Track Changes feature.

- JotSpot
www.jot.com

JotSpot allows users to simultaneously edit documents. The interface is clean and easy to use. Invited users can drag paragraphs to different areas of the document and edit text. Formatting options are very basic, and currently there is no method for keeping track of changes, although this might change given the site's recent acquisition by Google. This resource is ideal for live, collaborative note taking.

11

GENERATING AND TESTING HYPOTHESES

Although we most often think about *generating and testing hypotheses* in the context of science concepts, this strategy is applicable to all content areas. When students generate and test hypotheses, they are engaging in complex mental processes, applying content knowledge like facts and vocabulary, and enhancing their overall understanding of the content.

McREL's research on generating and testing hypotheses supports the following generalizations:

GENERALIZATIONS

1. The generating and testing of hypotheses can be approached in an inductive or deductive manner.
2. Teachers should ask students to clearly explain their hypotheses and their conclusions.

Based on these findings, we have two recommendations for classroom practice:

RECOMMENDATIONS

1. Make sure students can explain their hypotheses and conclusions.
2. Use a variety of structured tasks to guide students through generating and testing hypotheses.

The six tasks that teachers can use to help students generate and test hypotheses are (1) systems analysis, (2) problem solving, (3) historical investigation, (4) invention, (5) experimental inquiry, and (6) decision making.

1. In a *systems analysis,* students study the parts of a system, such as the ecosystem, and make predictions about what would change if one or more parts, such as a certain species of animal, were altered or removed.

2. When students *problem solve,* they look at various solutions given the obstacles and restraints posed by the problem.

3. In a *historical investigation,* students construct hypotheses about historical events for which there is no agreed-upon resolution.

4. Students involved in *invention* examine a need, then work to create a solution to the need.

5. *Experimental inquiry* often happens naturally when students observe a phenomenon, make an informed hypothesis about why or how that event happened, and set up an experiment to test their prediction.

6. Finally, when students are involved in *decision making,* they define criteria and apply weight to the various criteria to decide which choice makes the most sense.

Technology can play a vital role in generating and testing hypotheses because new developments in probeware and interactive applets allow students to spend more time *interpreting* the data rather than *gathering* the data—a process that can be tedious and error prone. In this section, we show how the following technologies significantly enhance the classroom practice of generating and testing hypotheses: *spreadsheet software, data collection tools,* and *Web resources.* Note that within each of these examples we present, the teacher is employing one of the six processes associated with generating and testing hypotheses. When teachers vary the processes in their classrooms, they are following the classroom recommendation that their students be engaged in different types of hypothesis generation.

○ Spreadsheet Software

Although the primary software for spreadsheets is Microsoft Excel, online collaborative spreadsheet software programs such as Google Spreadsheets and wikiCalc are becoming more widely used. Using spreadsheets to generate and test hypotheses is already common in science class, with students making informed predictions, collecting data, analyzing the data for patterns, and revising their original hypothesis or coming up with a new one. But what about spreadsheet uses in other subjects?

Even though setting up a spreadsheet is worthy technology skill for students to learn, content-area teachers don't want to use class time teaching students how to create spreadsheets; they want to use spreadsheets to help students learn the content. Let's look at an example of a teacher-created interactive spreadsheet that achieves this purpose. We should note that by calling the spreadsheet *interactive,* we mean that the students will be able to manipulate it, consider graphical patterns, and test their predictions by receiving quick feedback on multiple scenarios. To help students meet the district's economics benchmark in the social studies standards, Mrs. Omar sets a learning objective for her 5th grade class to understand savings, investments, and interest rates. Her goal is not to teach students about the mathematics or graphing skills involved; those are secondary learning outcomes in her subject. Instead, she wants students to learn that compounding interest and saving money can lead to strong earnings over time. Later, she will have her students apply this new knowledge to an understanding of how savings and investments affect the nation's economy.

With her goal set, Mrs. Omar designs an interactive spreadsheet that will show students the results of savings and investment options. She gives her students a scenario in which they have inherited $10,000 from a long-lost relative. She assigns students to small groups to discuss what they would do with the money and explains three plans they should consider for making money from an investment:

1. Spend $9,000 of the money right away but save the remaining $1,000 in a typical savings account that earns 4 percent annual interest. Deposit another $1,000 of your own money into the account each year for 30 years. Make a prediction of how much money you would earn on your total investment of $30,000 over 30 years.
2. Invest the whole $10,000 in a "safe" fund from Standard & Poor's 500 mutual fund index that earns an average of 8 percent per year. No further investments are made, but no money can be taken out of the account for 30 years. Make a prediction of how much money you would earn on your one time investment of $10,000 after 30 years.
3. Invest in a more unpredictable portfolio of diversified stocks from the Dow Jones Industrial Average, which has historically earned an average of 12 percent per year. Make a prediction of how much money you would earn on your one time investment of $10,000 after 30 years.

After students have reviewed the three plans, Mrs. Omar distributes a laptop computer to each small group. She asks them to locate their class folder on the school's network drive and open the spreadsheet document that she has created and saved for this activity. When the students open the document, they see a template that looks like Figure 11.1.

Figure 11.1
Interactive Savings and Investment Spreadsheet
Created in Microsoft Excel

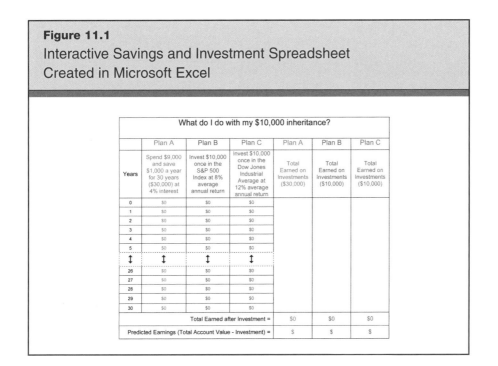

Before the students begin manipulating data, Mrs. Omar gives them a brief explanation of investment risk and prompts them to discuss the plan options in their groups and fill in their predictions for all three plans, regardless of which plan they favor. Then she asks each student to choose a plan and quickly takes a visual poll of the class's preferences for later comparison. Next she tells them to fill in the amounts in the Year 0 row. They can choose the scenario values of $1,000, $10,000, and $10,000 for Plans A, B, and C, or they can make up their own amounts. Because the spreadsheet is interactive, any value will produce results to compare to students' initial predictions. All they have to do is put numbers in the first row. The interactive formulation of the spreadsheet does the rest, filling in the table and mapping data on a chart, as shown in Figures 11.2 and 11.3.

Figure 11.2

Interactive Savings and Investment Spreadsheet: Example Projections

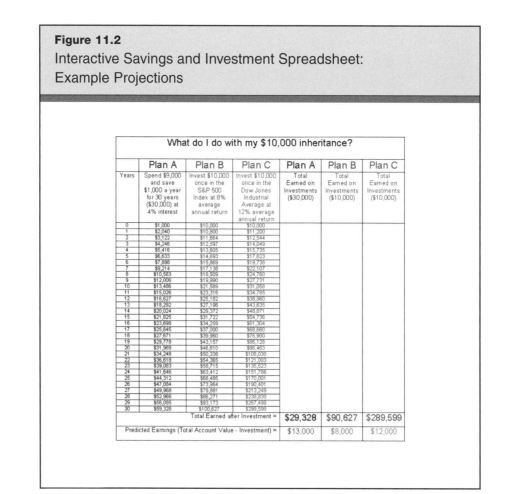

	What do I do with my $10,000 inheritance?					
	Plan A	Plan B	Plan C	Plan A	Plan B	Plan C
Years	Spend $9,000 and save $1,000 a year for 30 years ($30,000) at 4% interest	Invest $10,000 once in the S&P 500 Index at 8% average annual return	Invest $10,000 once in the Dow Jones Industrial Average at 12% average annual return	Total Earned on Investments ($30,000)	Total Earned on Investments ($10,000)	Total Earned on Investments ($10,000)
0	$1,000	$10,000	$10,000			
1	$2,040	$10,800	$11,200			
2	$3,122	$11,664	$12,544			
3	$4,246	$12,597	$14,049			
4	$5,416	$13,605	$15,735			
5	$6,633	$14,693	$17,623			
6	$7,898	$15,869	$19,738			
7	$9,214	$17,138	$22,107			
8	$10,583	$18,509	$24,760			
9	$12,006	$19,990	$27,731			
10	$13,486	$21,589	$31,058			
11	$15,026	$23,316	$34,785			
12	$16,627	$25,182	$38,960			
13	$18,292	$27,196	$43,635			
14	$20,024	$29,372	$48,871			
15	$21,825	$31,722	$54,736			
16	$23,698	$34,259	$61,304			
17	$25,645	$37,000	$68,660			
18	$27,671	$39,960	$76,900			
19	$29,778	$43,157	$86,128			
20	$31,969	$46,610	$96,463			
21	$34,248	$50,338	$108,038			
22	$36,618	$54,365	$121,003			
23	$39,083	$58,715	$135,523			
24	$41,646	$63,412	$151,786			
25	$44,312	$68,485	$170,001			
26	$47,084	$73,964	$190,401			
27	$49,968	$79,881	$213,249			
28	$52,966	$86,271	$238,839			
29	$56,085	$93,173	$267,499			
30	$59,328	$100,627	$299,599			
			Total Earned after Investment =	$29,328	$90,627	$289,599
		Predicted Earnings (Total Account Value - Investment) =		$13,000	$8,000	$12,000

Using the teacher-created interactive spreadsheet, students can compare their predictions to actual results without spending lots of valuable time doing calculations or designing spreadsheets. They can enter many different monetary amounts and see the results in an instant. This helps them see patterns, such as exponential growth. A mathematics teacher might decide to use the same lesson to focus on the compounding percentage calculations and exponential patterns. In either case, the teacher is using technology to maximize instructional time and meet learning objectives. This spreadsheet activity allows students to gain a deeper understanding of investment basics and requires them to use their critical thinking skills to predict outcomes. Students generate and test hypotheses in very little time and gain valuable experience that they can apply to future economic hypotheses. When Mrs. Omar asks her students to present their findings, she is following the classroom recommendation of ensuring that students can articulate their hypotheses.

Figure 11.3
Interactive Savings and Investment Chart:
Example Projections

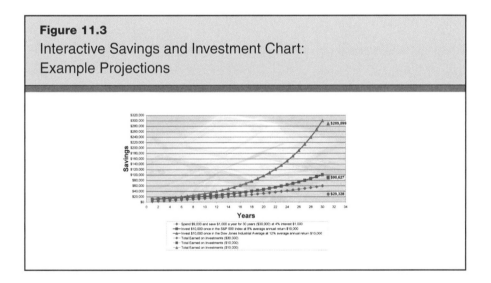

How did Mrs. Omar create her interactive spreadsheet? She began by testing her own hypotheses to see what scenarios would work best. Then she put multiple formulas in the cells at the *fx* prompt that would calculate the different interest rates and totals, as seen in Figure 11.4.

She did not have to program a formula into each cell through row 32. Once she had programmed the first cells (B5, C5, and D5) she just

Figure 11.4

Interactive Savings and Investment Spreadsheet Stage 1:
Cell Formula Programming for Compounding Interest

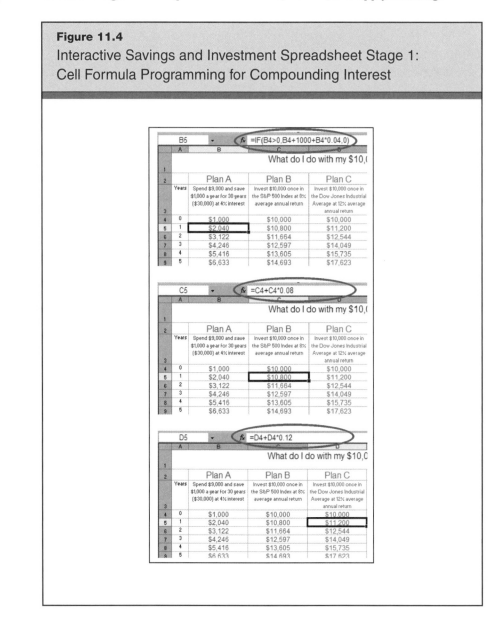

highlighted the cell's formula by placing her mouse at the bottom right corner of the cell and dragging to highlight the column down to cell 32, as shown in Figure 11.5. This copies the formula format in all the cells with the correct column and row designation.

Next, she entered formulas (e.g., *fx*=(B34>0, B34-30000, "$0") to show how much was earned on the total investments by taking the total earned in row 34 and subtracting the invested money (either $30,000 or $10,000) for each of the three plans (see Figure 11.6).

Figure 11.5

Interactive Savings and Investment Spreadsheet Stage 2:
Cell Formula Copy Programming for Compounding Interest

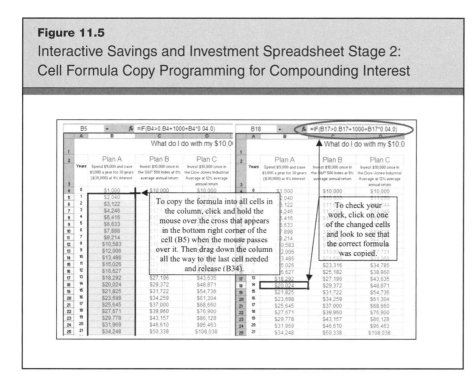

Figure 11.6

Interactive Savings and Investment Spreadsheet Stage 3:
Cell Formula Programming for Totals Earned

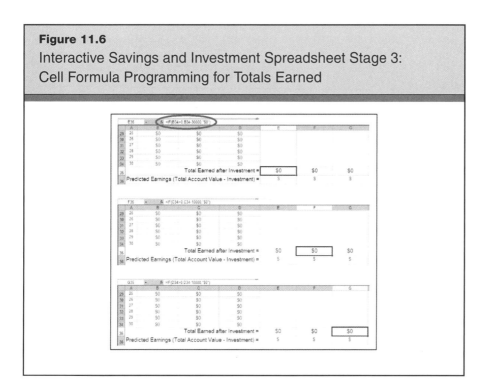

Finally, she inserted some numbers and created a line-graph chart. Then she highlighted the numbers and chart when students entered amounts in the first row. Mrs. Omar does allow her students to save their own spreadsheets from the template and add any color schemes they like. For more information on how to formulate cells and create templates, go to http://office.microsoft.com and follow the site's Help and How-to links.

○ Data Collection Tools

Collecting data usually answers some questions and generates new ones. Typically, students research a problem, form a hypothesis, and collect data to confirm, deny, or revise their last hypothesis. This cycle of inquiry can be repeated many times. Using data collection tools enables students to see the bigger picture and recognize patterns. As we noted in Chapter 5's focus on nonlinguistic representation, digital probes and microscopes facilitate analysis, synthesis, and problem solving. By and large, science teachers are the most likely to use probes and digital microscopes, but resourceful teachers in all subjects can incorporate these tools in ways that will enhance the curriculum. For example, art students could use a light intensity probe to examine the interplay of light and color in great works of art, and history students could use a digital microscope to record detailed images from an archeological excavation and gain further insight into an ancient culture.

Now let's look more closely at what we mean when we say that a data collection tool can enhance learning. Mrs. Schwartz's middle school science class has heard rumors that their community gets acid rainfall. Is this true? Students would like to know. The class decides to research acid rain as part of their studies in chemical reactions and meteorology. They find that "acid rain" is acidic rain, snow, fog, and dew. Distilled water has a neutral pH of 7. Liquids with a pH less than 7 are acidic, and those with a pH greater than 7 are basic. "Clean" or unpolluted rain has a moderately acidic pH of 5.6, because carbon dioxide and water in the air react together to form carbonic acid that combines with the moisture in the air. Based on these facts, the students decide to find out if their rain is more acidic than normal and focus on what this might mean for their local environment.

Mrs. Schwartz helps her students devise a plan to use a USB connectable data probe to collect pH readings from various water sources in the community to compare with the 5.6 pH of normal rain water. Before they begin collecting data, students predict the pH of the various sources. Figure 11.7 shows their predictions.

Figure 11.7
Digital Probe Activity: Water pH Predictions

Water Source	Predicted pH
Rain	5.0
Pond	5.0
River	6.0
Stream	5.0
Tap	7.0

After collecting data with a digital pH probe from the various samples, students quickly create a chart like the one in Figure 11.8. When they compare the data to their predictions, students are surprised find that the pH of their rain is even more acidic than predicted. They also are puzzled by the differences among their various water sources. For instance, why was the pond water so much more acidic than the river water? And what does this mean for the life that depends on these waters? The data collection tool allows Mrs. Schwartz's class to gather and graph data quickly and accurately, leaving more time for analysis and synthesis. Their findings lead to further hypotheses and more inquiry.

Data collection tools are not always probes. The Internet is a huge data collection tool. To expand their inquiry to a larger scale, Mrs. Schwartz's students could share and compare their data online through collaborative project Web sites such as the Global Schoolhouse (www.globalschoolnet.org) or the Collaboratory Project (http://collaboratory.nunet.net). Sharing and comparing data from other localities gives students enough information to generate and test hypotheses concerning the nation and other parts of the world.

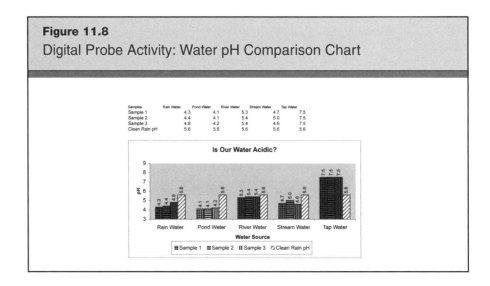

Figure 11.8
Digital Probe Activity: Water pH Comparison Chart

As a side note, this example perfectly illustrations how technological applications help teachers to combine the instructional strategies that affect student achievement. How many of the nine instructional strategies does this activity feature? By our count, at least four:

1. Identifying similarities and differences, when students compare their data.

2. Nonlinguistic representation, when students present these data as a graph.

3. Generating and testing hypotheses, when students predict the pH levels of water samples based on sample source and the proximity of industry.

4. Using questions, cues, and advance organizers, when the students and teacher discuss what pH is and why it's important to know the pH levels of the water they use.

○ Web Resources

Web resources and gaming software, in the form of interactive applets and simulations, allow students to use background knowledge, make decisions, and see the outcome of their hypotheses, often in virtual situations that would be impossible or financially unfeasible in real life. Simulation software also can provide incredibly engaging learning environments, resulting in increased motivation and retention in learning.

Consider the example of Dave McDivitt, a high school history teacher at Oak Hill High School in Converse, Indiana, who decided to use a historically accurate World War II multiplayer strategy game to help his students better understand the political and economic causes and conditions that led to the war. Muzzy Lane's Making History: The Calm and the Storm (see Figure 11.9) is available at www. making-history.com and includes features specifically designed to facilitate classroom use.

Figure 11.9
Screen Shot of Making History Multiplayer Strategy Game

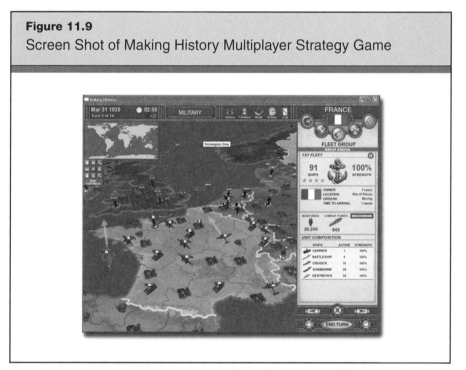

Reproduced courtesy of Muzzy Lane Software Inc.

Each student takes on the role of a country leader and makes policy decisions about diplomacy, economics, domestic matters, and military actions to achieve that country's goals. Actually, Dave McDivitt set up an experiment: using the game in one class and teaching another class the same material using more traditional methods. Those students using the simulation software not only recorded higher test scores but also—and perhaps more important—showed overwhelming enthusiasm while learning the material. "Leaders" of the different countries were overheard in hallways and between classes strategizing and planning.

You can read about Mr. McDivitt's experiences on Serious Gamers Source (http://seriousgamessource.com/features/feature_051606.php) and on his blog at http://davidmcdivitt.wordpress.com. His blog includes student quotes on the experience, data from test scores, and his own perspective as the teacher. You can also read more in Muzzy Lane's May 9, 2006, press release at www.muzzylane.com/news/detail.php?id=79.

In the list of resources that follows, we also include a few software applications that can be ordered online.

- Smog City
www.smogcity.com

This resource engages students in a systems analysis by allowing them to set parameters for weather, population, and emissions, and then showing them the variable effects on a city's ozone levels.

- NASA SCIence Files Problem Board
http://whyfiles.larc.nasa.gov/treehouse.html

This resource from NASA has a rich infrastructure to guide teachers and students through problem-solving activities. Older problem boards are text-based, while newer ones have Flash components, but both have excellent activities. Students solve "cases" while learning critical thinking and problem-solving skills. Included are resources to help teachers directly instruct the problem-solving process as students solve the mystery.

- NOVA Building Big
www.pbs.org/wgbh/buildingbig

This resource helps students learn about bridges, domes, skyscrapers, dams, and tunnels. In each activity, students apply what they have learned to solve problems related to a fictional city's needs by deciding which structure is best for each situation.

- Plimoth Plantation's You Are the Historian
www.plimoth.org/education/olc/index_js2.html

This very in-depth historical investigation helps students use primary sources in order to distinguish fact from lore about the first Thanksgiving. Students actively investigate remaining sources that exist from 1621 in order to make hypotheses about what actually happened.

- PrimaryAccess
www.primaryaccess.org

You can incorporate this resource into a historical inquiry to help students use primary-source images to create movies about a historical event. Similar to other movie-editing software, PrimaryAccess scaffolds the storytelling process for students.

- By Kids for Kids: How to Invent
www.bkfk.com/howtoinvent

This Web site introduces children to the invention process, including thinking about how to solve problems and finding out if someone else has already had the same idea.

- Invention Web Resources
www.pendergast.k12.az.us/schools/cbreeze/pepclass/inventions/
inventions.htm

This site is a vast collection of invention resources including Web-Quests and various historical links about inventions.

- Darwin Pond
www.ventrella.com/Darwin/darwin.html

Darwin Pond is an experimental inquiry game that allows students to create and evolve "swimmers" by tweaking such characteristics as their color, speed of swimming, and number of joints in legs. Once the swimmers are created, the student can watch to see what happens or continue to modify the environment and make predictions about the effect the changes will have.

- Practicing with the Catapult
www.lcse.umn.edu/specs/labs/catapult/practice.html

This experimental inquiry game allows students to adjust a catapult's height, projectile velocity, launch angle, and other factors. The student must predict how the variables will affect the catapult's ability to land a hit on a building.

- Zoo Matchmaker
www.minnesotazoo.org/education/games/matchmaker

This resource from the Minnesota Zoo helps students learn about the decisions that zookeepers need to make in order to control diseases while keeping the genetic pool diverse.

- Windward!
www.ciconline.org/windward

This game helps students learn about weather and wind patterns across the world's oceans and then asks them to use that knowledge to navigate a ship around the world.

- Hurricane Strike!
http://meted.ucar.edu/hurrican/strike/index.htm

This simulation from the University Corporation for Atmospheric Research in Boulder, Colorado, takes students through tutorials about hurricanes and helps them apply what they've learned to make decisions as a hurricane approaches.

- ExploreLearning
www.explorelearning.com

Using the interactive manipulatives known as gizmos, students can generate and test hypotheses on a number of subjects: the genetic makeup of mice, balancing chemical equations, comparing and ordering fractions, and estimating population sizes, to name just a few.

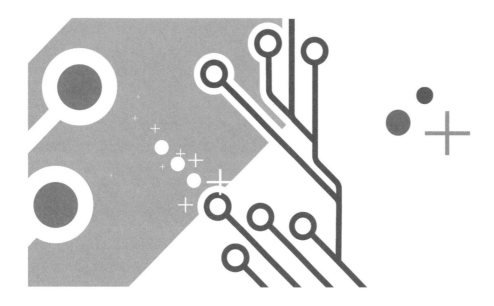

Appendix:
Planning for Technology

Using technology for technology's sake isn't a good application of instructional time or funding, and it is unlikely to improve student achievement. It is essential that teachers design a quality lesson plan first and then select the most appropriate technologies to support that lesson.

The Four Planning Questions

In the Introduction, we discussed the four planning questions for instruction:

1. What will students learn?
2. Which strategies will provide evidence of student learning?
3. Which strategies will help students acquire and integrate learning?
4. Which strategies will help students practice, review, and apply learning?

Your lesson design should *always* begin here.

What Will Students Learn?

To answer Question 1, you must look to your state standards and district-level benchmarks or indicators. Which content standards and indicators are you going to address with this lesson? After finding your answer, determine the technology standards and indicators that complement the content standards. Some districts have specific, self-developed technology standards, but most districts use standards aligned with the National Educational Technology Standards for Students (NETS-S), developed by the International Society for Technology in Education (ISTE). The complete NETS-S document is online at http://cnets.iste.org/currstands/cstands-netss.html. In addition to the student technology standards, ISTE and NCREL developed an achievement rubric for the NETS-S standards. This document is online at www.ncrel.org/tech/nets/p-12rubric.pdf.

The primary instructional strategy identified for the first planning question is *setting objectives*. As the teacher, your task is to think about how you will determine and activate your students' prior knowledge. How will students personalize their learning goals? Are you going to create an online survey? Do you need to reserve a computer lab or mobile cart?

Which Strategies Will Provide Evidence of Student Learning?

Now that you have selected your content standards and benchmarks and have identified the technology standard or standards you are going to address, it is time to consider the teaching strategies that will let you know that your students have mastered or are mastering the content. The instructional strategies most relevant to this question are *providing feedback* and *providing recognition*.

At this point in the planning process, it is important to determine how your students will demonstrate their learning. The way students will demonstrate learning shouldn't be an afterthought; it should drive the lesson design. For example, if you have determined that students will be doing a presentation on a topic, what will the rubric for the presentation look like? Will the presentation be a three- or four-person cooperative project, pair work, or individual work? Will it involve a PowerPoint presentation or a student-created video? Is there an online WebQuest that meets your learning goals? Answers to these questions begin to shape the lesson and help you select the right technologies to support the lesson.

Which Strategies Will Help Students Acquire and Integrate Learning?

The teaching strategies most relevant to Question 3 are *cues, questions, and advance organizers; nonlinguistic representation; summarizing and note taking, cooperative learning;* and *reinforcing effort.* It's at this stage of the planning process that many teachers find technology most powerful. What will your advance organizer look like? What summary frame or frames will be most appropriate? Are you going to use a combination notes template? How can you use technology to reinforce your students' effort? What Web resources are most appropriate to help students acquire knowledge? Are there videos on United Streaming that you should download in advance? Are there any ExploreLearning gizmos you might use? Do you want to bookmark sites on individual computers or set up a del.icio.us site on the Web to organize and share your bookmarks?

Also note that it is during this phase in the planning process that the power of using technology to differentiate instruction is most evident. Teachers differentiate instruction by modifying the depth or complexity of content, the processes by which students learn, the content itself, and the products students are expected to create, based on considerations of learning styles, interests, and skill levels (Tomlinson & Eidson, 2003). A teacher who incorporates technology greatly expands the pool of resources, means of instructional presentation and support, and modes of product creation available to students, and is thus better equipped to meet varying student needs. For example, visual learners and aural learners might be more engaged by a BrainPop movie on balancing algebraic equations, while kinesthetic learners might connect better to the same information by "handling" virtual manipulatives at the National Library of Virtual Manipulatives. Students in both groups might watch or listen just once before going on to explore the content at a more sophisticated level with the help of an ExploreLearning gizmo, or they might watch or listen multiple times. They might replay the entire movie or sound file or just certain segments.

Which Strategies Will Help Students Practice, Review, and Apply Learning?

The strategies identified under Question 4 are *homework and practice, identifying similarities and differences,* and *generating and testing hypotheses.* Remember that practice should be focused and that students need to practice a new skill 24 times on average to reach 80-percent mastery. What are the multiple ways you are going to provide for students to practice a new skill? Are there Web sites students can access from home that will help with practice? Is it appropriate in this lesson to use Inspiration to compare and contrast? Can students create analogies to deepen their understanding of the topic? Are there simulations available online to allow students to generate and test hypotheses about the topic?

A Template for Lesson Planning with Technology

To help teachers plan for technology effectively, we have developed the McREL Technology Solutions (MTS) Lesson Plan Template, shown in Figure A.1.

Complete the MTS Lesson Plan Template as you address the four planning questions. The answer to *"What knowledge will students learn?"* provides the brief lesson description, district content standard/benchmark addressed, and NETS-S standard addressed. The answer to *"Which strategies will provide evidence that students have learned that knowledge?"* should go in the assessment method box. The answers to the third and fourth questions, *"Which strategies will help students acquire and integrate the knowledge?"* and *"Which strategies will help students practice, review, and apply the knowledge?"* go in both the technology resources needed and procedure boxes.

Jeff Davidson, a 7th grade teacher, used combination notes to teach mitosis in his science class. Figure A.2 is his completed MTS Lesson Plan for that unit. The lesson culminated with an assignment for students to create their own combination notes-style PowerPoint presentation on the topic: a slide featuring at least five facts, two downloaded pictures, a voice recording explaining one of the pictures, a movie or animation, and a two-sentence written summary.

Figure A.1
McREL Technology Solutions (MTS) Lesson Plan Template

Name: _____

Subject area: _____

Grade level: _____

Lesson title: _____

Brief lesson description

District content standard/benchmark addressed

NETS-S technology standard addressed

Technology resources needed (hardware and software)

Procedure

Assessment method

Figure A.2
Lesson Plan Created with the MTS Lesson Plan Template

Name: Jeff Davidson
Subject area: Life Science
Grade level: 7th grade
Lesson title: Mitosis Combination Notes

Brief lesson description

The students use their textbook, the Internet, outside resources, and notes to get background knowledge about the process of mitosis. The students then use PowerPoint to present this information in multimedia format (using movie clips, animations, sounds, voice, and pictures). Each student presents his or her PowerPoint panels to the class.

District content standard/benchmark addressed

1. (c) Use appropriate tools, mathematics, technology, and techniques to gather, analyze, and interpret data.
2. (b) Conduct research.
    (e) Possess technical skills: Read/write/present. Use technology (PowerPoint, Internet, search tools).
4. Understand that the cell is the basic unit of life.
    (c) Understand the role of cell division, reproduction, and heredity for all living things.
    (d) Differentiate between asexual and sexual reproduction in plants and animals.

NETS-S technology standard addressed

1. Basic operations and concepts
3. Technology productivity tools
5. Technology research tools

Technology resources needed (hardware and software)

Computers with Internet access, microphones, speakers/headphones
PowerPoint software (with prepared template), multimedia software (Real Player One, Windows Media Player, etc.)

Procedure

Introduction: The students completed the unit on Cells and Parts of a Cell prior to this lesson. They also have experience using combination notes.
Activity: The students use outside resources along with their notes and textbook to find information about mitosis and cell division, presented in text, voice, pictures, and movie/animation form. Next, students place this information, in the form of combination notes, in a PowerPoint presentation.
Technology Integration: The students use a teacher-designed PowerPoint template to present their information. The students will find their information using the Internet and search engines in addition to their normal resources (books and notes). This wider range of resources will allow each student to present different information, exposing the class as a whole to various takes on the topic. The students will also use a microphone to insert recordings of their voice into their PowerPoint presentations to explain particular pictures or facts. They will use headphones to listen to their voices during the recording process and to find other sounds that will help explain their information.

Assessment method

Students will be assessed using a rubric based on a 10 point–5 point–1 point scale. Criteria will include (1) use of color/formatting so that the slide is attractive and legible; (2) quality and completeness of the content presented (see content standard/benchmark); (3) use of picture/movies/animation to convey key points; (4) participation; (5) quality and clarity of the sketched out/written rough draft.

Rights and Permissions

Today's technology makes it easier than ever for students to copy and use digital content, including copyrighted material. (Fortunately, teachers can use the same technology to identify when plagiarism has taken place by searching for exact words on the Web.) It is important for teachers to model *and* monitor adherence to copyright laws and to demonstrate best practices for being a part of "digital citizenship." We encourage you to teach your students about fair use and copyright laws. For more information, see "Technology & Learning's Copyright and Fair Use Guidelines for Teachers," available at www.techlearning.com. Click on Hot Topics > Copyright.

Internet Safety

Throughout this book we advocate instructional use of blogs, wikis, e-mail, instant messaging, and other forms of technologies that some consider inappropriate in a school setting. Some of the objections arise from legitimate concern about student safety. Yes, there are Internet predators. Yes, it is possible that students will go off topic while chatting. Yes, there are Internet sites that are inappropriate for kids—and for most adults, for that matter.

As we see it, schools have two choices: to ban any form of online communication that might present a potential danger, or to teach appropriate and ethical use of the technology. It is our opinion that schools should be proactive rather than reactive in this area, which is why we advocate the second choice. If schools ban online technologies, they are also banning valuable teaching tools. In addition, teachers lose the opportunity to engage students in much-needed conversations about keeping safe online. These conversations need to occur because students will use these technologies personally, whether schools ban them or not. The Internet exists outside of the walls of your classroom; your students need and deserve your guidance in this area.

Child predators are nothing new. We teach our students at an early age how to react if a stranger approaches them on the way home from school. We teach our students about appropriate and inappropriate touch. We do this because we acknowledge that there are inherent dangers in the world, and our children are more likely to be safe if we arm them with knowledge. The complication when it comes to educating our children about the dangers inherent in the Internet is that we adults don't understand the online world quite as well as we understand walking to and from school, going to the park to play with friends, and answering the door when parents aren't at home. Because most of us don't have a blog or an instant message account, we don't know how they work or what purpose they might serve. Here are some good resources to get you started:

• *Blogs, Wikis, Podcasts, and Other Powerful Web Tools for Classrooms* by Will Richardson

• *Classroom Blogging: A Teacher's Guide to the Blogosphere* by David Warlick

• *Redefining Literacy for the 21st Century* by David Warlick

Schools can play a much-needed role in Internet safety by providing rules for online behavior and then by monitoring those activities. Just as we teach students never to give out personal information on the phone, we should teach them that that there are some things that are inappropriate for them to reveal online. Just as we teach students to scream and run away if a stranger approaches them in the park, we should teach them to close an online chat window and report inappropriate conversations to an adult. Just as students must learn that it is wrong to be a bully on the playground or to pass hurtful notes, they must learn that cyber-bullying is wrong and won't be tolerated. They also need to know why and how to forward any inappropriate messages to the proper authorities.

The set-up of a classroom or computer lab goes a long way in helping to monitor appropriate and inappropriate online behavior. Computer screens should be visible to the teacher. Arranging computer workstations in a ring against the outer walls of a lab or classroom with the screens facing the center of the room is much more conducive to monitoring than setting up rows of computers with many of the screens hidden from the teacher's view. Students need to know that when they log into their computer, there is an electronic record of their transaction that can be traced back to them, both at school and at home.

Finally, while filtering programs are generally effective, there will still be inappropriate sites that might make it to the screen. Teach your students that if they inadvertently come to an inappropriate site, they should click the window closed and tell an adult. If they repeatedly "inadvertently" come to an inappropriate site, they will be held accountable. This is really no different from a situation like middle school students bringing inappropriate material to school in their backpacks.

•°+ References

Adam, K. P. (2001). *Computerized scoring of essays for analytical writing assessments: Evaluating score validity.* Seattle, WA: National Council on Measurement in Education. (ERIC Document Reproduction Service No. ED 458296)

Alexander, B. (March/April 2006). Web 2.0: A new wave of innovation for teaching and learning? *Educause.* Retrieved April 25, 2006, from http://www.educause.edu/ir/library/pdf/erm0621.pdf

Anderson, L. W., & Krathwohl, D. R. (Eds.). (2001). *A taxonomy for learning, teaching, and assessing: A revision of Bloom's taxonomy of educational objectives.* New York: Longman.

Ausubel, D. P. (1960). The use of advance organizers in the learning and retention of meaningful verbal material. *Journal of Educational Psychology, 51,* 267–272.

Barley, Z., Lauer, P. A., Arens, S. A., Apthorp, H. S., Englert, K. S., Snow, D., & Akiba, M. (2002). *Helping at-risk students meet standards: A synthesis of evidence-based classroom practices.* Denver, CO: Mid-continent Research for Education and Learning.

Black, S. (2001, May). Ask me a question. *American School Board Journal, 188*(5), 43.

Brabec, K., Fisher, K., & Pitler, H. (2004, February). Building better instruction: How technology supports nine research-proven instructional strategies. *Learning and Leading with Technology, 31*(5), 6–11.

Cholmsky, P. (2003). *Why gizmos work: Empirical evidence for the instructional effectiveness of ExploreLearning's interactive content.* Charlottesville, VA: ExploreLearning. Retrieved March 15, 2006, from http://www.explorelearning.com/View/downloads/WhyGizmosWork.pdf

Cochran, D., Conklin, J., & Modin, S. (2007, February). A new Bloom: Transforming learning. *Learning and Leading with Technology, 34*(5), 22–25.

Consortium of College and University Media Centers. (1996). *Fair Use Guidelines for Educational Multimedia.* Washington, DC: Author. Available: http://www. utsystem.edu/ogc/intellectualproperty/ccmcguid.htm.

Dodge, B., & March, T. (1995). *What is a WebQuest?* Retrieved April 26, 2006, from http://webquest.sdsu.edu/overview.htm

Fico, M. (2005, June 1). Honoring student's voices. *Educator's eZine.* Retrieved March 17, 2006, from http://www.techlearning.com/story/showArticle. jhtml?articleID=163105484

Friedman, T. L. (2005). *The world is flat: A brief history of the twenty-first century.* New York: Farrar, Straus, and Giroux.

Goodwyn, B. (1999, June). Improving teaching quality: Issues & policies [Policy brief]. Denver, CO: Mid-continent Research for Education and Learning. Retrieved April 10, 2006, from http://www.mcrel.org/PDF/PolicyBriefs/ 5983PI_PBImprovingTeacherQuality.pdf

Halverson, R. (2005). What can K–12 school leaders learn from video games and gaming? *Innovate, 1*(6). Retrieved March 14, 2006, from http://www. innovateonline.info/index.php?view=article&id=81

Hattie, J. A. (1992). Measuring the effects of schooling. *Australian Journal of Education, 36*(1), 9.

High schools plug into online writing program: MYAccess! boosts end-of-year scores. (2003, November 1). *District Administrator, 39*(11). Retrieved March 14, 2006, from http://www.districtadministration.com/page.cfm?p=572

Hill, J., & Flynn, K. (2006). *Classroom instruction that works with English language learners.* Alexandria, VA: Association for Supervision and Curriculum Development.

Hom Jr., H. L., & Murphy, M. D. (1983, November). Low need achievers' performance: The positive impact of a self-directed goal. *Personality and Social Psychology Bulletin*, 11, 275–285.

Johnson, D. W., Johnson, R. T., & Stanne, M. B. (2000). *Cooperative learning methods: A meta-analysis.* Minneapolis, MN: University of Minnesota. Retrieved May 4, 2006, from http://www.co-operation.org/pages/cl-methods.html

Klopfer, E. (July/August 2005). Playing to learn: State-of-the-art computer games go to school. *Access Learning.* Retrieved March 14, 2006, from http://www. ciconline.org/cicmagazine-jul_aug05

Kriz, W., & Eberle, T. (2004). *Bridging the gap: Transforming knowledge into action through gaming and simulation.* Proceedings of the 35th Conference of the International Simulation and Gaming Association (ISAGA). Munich, Germany.

Kulik, J. A., & Kulik, C. C. (1988). Timing of feedback and verbal learning. *Review of Educational Research, 58,* 79–97.

Lobel, J. (2006). Multiplayer computer gaming simulations facilitating cooperative learning. IT in Education, Trinity College Dublin. Available: https://www.cs. tcd.ie/~lobelj/portfolio/literature_review/literature_review_jonathan_lobel. pdf

Lucas, G. (2005, November 17). George Lucas and the new world of learning [Podcast]. *Edutopia Radio Show.* Retrieved August 28, 2006, from http://www. edutopia.org/php/radio.php

Marzano, R. J. (1998). *A theory-based meta-analysis of research on instruction.* Aurora, CO: Mid-continent Research for Education and Learning. Retrieved February 7, 2006, from http://www.mcrel.org/instructionmetaanalysis

Marzano, R. J., & Kendall, J. S. (2007). *The new taxonomy of educational objectives* (2nd ed.). Thousand Oaks, CA: Corwin.

Marzano, R. J., Pickering, D. J., & Pollock, J. E. (2001). *Classroom instruction that works: Research-based strategies for increasing student achievement.* Alexandria, VA: Association of Supervision and Curriculum Development.

Mize, C. D., & Gibbons, A. (2000). More than inventory: Effective integration of instructional technology to support student learning in K–12 schools. (ERIC Document Reproduction Service No. ED 444563)

Page, M. S. (2002, Summer). Technology-enriched classrooms: Effects on students of low socioeconomic status. *Journal of Research on Technology in Education, 34*(4), 389–409.

Palincsar, A. S., & Brown, A. L. (1984). Reciprocal teaching of comprehension-fostering and comprehension-monitoring activities. *Cognition and Instruction, 1*(2), 117–175. Available: http://www.garfield.library.upenn.edu/classics1993/A1993LU43900001.pdf

Palincsar, A. S., & Brown, A. L. (1985). Reciprocal teaching: Activities to promote reading with your mind. In T. L. Harris and E. J. Cooper (Eds.), *Reading, thinking, and concept development: Strategies for the classroom.* New York: The College Board.

Prensky, M. (2000). *Digital game-based learning.* New York: McGraw-Hill.

Reeves, T. (1998). *The impact of media and technology in schools*: Research report for The Bertelsmann Foundation. Athens, GA: The University of Georgia. Retrieved March 30, 2006, from http://it.coe.uga.edu/~treeves/edit6900/BertelsmannReeves98.pdf

Ringstaff, C., & Kelley, L. (2002). *The learning return on our education technology investment: A review of findings from research.* San Francisco: WestEd RTEC.

Russell, J., & Sorge, D. (1999). Training facilitators to enhance technology integration. *Journal of Instruction Delivery Systems, 13*(4), 6.

Schacter, J. (1999). *The impact of education technology on student achievement: What the most current research has to say.* Santa Monica, CA: Milken Exchange on Education Technology.

Schacter, J., & Fagnano, C. (1999). Does computer technology improve student learning and achievement? How, when, and under what conditions? *Journal of Educational Computing Research, 20*(4), 329–343.

Schunk, D. H. (2003). Self-efficacy for reading and writing: Influence of modeling, goal setting, and self-evaluation. *Reading & Writing Quarterly, 19,* 159–172.

Sedensky, M. (2005, May 5). Computers now grading students' writing: Essay-grading software increasingly being used on everything from routine papers to GMAT essay. Retrieved February 6, 2006, from http://sfgate.com/cgi-bin/article.cgi?file=/n/a/2005/05/09/national/a050818D46.DTL

Siegle, D., & Foster, T. (2000, April). Effects of laptop computers with multimedia and presentation software on student achievement. Paper presented at the meeting of the American Education Research Association (AERA), New Orleans, LA.

Squire, K. (2001). Reframing the cultural space of computer and video games. *Massachusetts Institute of Technology*. Retrieved March 14, 2006, from http://cms.mit.edu/games/education/research-vision.html

Surowiecki, J. (2004). *The wisdom of crowds: Why the many are smarter than the few and how collective wisdom shapes business, economies, societies, and nations*. New York: Doubleday.

Tomlinson, C. A., & Eidson, C. C. (2003). *Differentiation in practice: A resource guide for differentiating curriculum, grades K–5*. Alexandria, VA: Association for Supervision and Curriculum Development.

Tseng, C. H. (2004, August). Pupils' using of multimedia advance organizer and learning retention. In V. Uskov (Ed.), *Proceedings of Computers and Advanced Technology in Education, Kauai, Hawaii*. Calgary, Canada: ACTA Press. Article available for purchase at http://www.actapress.com/Content_Of_Proceeding. aspx?ProceedingID=261.

Urquhart, V., & McIver, M. (2005). *Teaching writing in the content areas*. Alexandria, VA: Association of Supervision and Curriculum Development; and Aurora, CO: McREL.

Waxman, H. C., Connell, M. L., & Gray, J. (2002). *A quantitative synthesis of recent research on the effects of teaching and learning with technology on student outcomes*. Naperville, IL: North Central Regional Educational Laboratory. Available: http://www.coe.ufl.edu/Courses/eme5054/Foundations/Articles/waxman.pdf

Wong, H. K., & Wong, R. T. (1998). *How to be an effective teacher: The first days of school*. Mountain View, CA: Harry K. Wong Publications, Inc.

Referenced Products

Adobe Photoshop® is a registered trademark of Adobe Systems Incorporated.

Adobe Premiere™ is a trademark of Adobe Systems Incorporated.

AIM™ is a trademark of America Online, Inc. (AOL).

Appleworks® is a registered trademark of Apple Inc.

Backpack™ is a trademark of 37signals LLC.

Blackboard Academic Suite™ is a trademark of Blackboard® Inc.

BrainStorm for Windows™ is a trademark of Brainstorm Software Ltd.

Campfire™ is a trademark of 37signals LLC.

ClassAct® is a registered trademark of the LJ Group LTD.

EduGame!™ is a trademark of Eduware Incorporated.

Excel® is a registered trademark of Microsoft Corporation.

Flash® is a registered trademark of Adobe Systems Incorporated.

FrontPage® is a registered trademark of Microsoft Corporation.

GarageBand™ is a trademark of Apple Inc.

Gmail™ is a trademark of Google Inc.

Google Spreadsheets™ is a trademark of Google Inc.

GraphicConverter™ is a trademark of Lemke Software GMBH.

Hotmail® is a registered trademark of Microsoft Corporation.

HyperStudio® is a registered trademark of Knowledge Adventure, Inc.

iChat™ is a trademark of Apple Computer Inc.

iMovie® is a registered trademark of Apple Inc.

●+ INDEX

Note: Figures are indicated with an italicized *f* following the page number.

·⁺ About the Authors

Howard Pitler is the Senior Director of Educational Technology for Mid-continent Research for Education and Learning (McREL) in Denver, Colorado. Dr. Pitler was a high school and middle school teacher for 10 years and an elementary and middle school principal for 15 years. While he was the principal of L'Ouverture Computer Technology Magnet Elementary in Wichita, Kansas, his school was named an Apple Distinguished Program, one of *Redbook*'s "Top 100 School in America," and one of *PC Magazine*'s "Top Wired Schools in America." He holds a doctorate and an educational specialist degree in Educational Administration and a master's degree in Musical Performance from Wichita State University, and a bachelor's degree in Music Education from Indiana State University. Dr. Pitler was named National Distinguished Principal in 1997 and is currently an Apple Distinguished Educator.

Elizabeth R. Hubbell is a Senior Educational Technology Consultant at McREL, where she facilitates workshops and provides consulting services in the areas of technology integration for schools and districts across the United States. Ms. Hubbell has nine years of experience as a teacher, with a background in Montessori education. She holds a master's degree in Information and Learning Technologies from the University of Colorado–Denver and a bachelor's degree in Early Childhood Education from the University of Georgia. Ms. Hubbell was one of four national finalists in *Technology & Learning*'s 2003 Ed Tech Leader of the Year, and she has served on the advisory board of PBS TeacherSource.

Matt Kuhn is a Senior Educational Technology Consultant for McREL. Before coming to McREL, he was an education programs manager with the National Renewable Energy Laboratory (NREL), where he educated teachers, students, and consumers about renewable energy science and technology, and received NREL's Technology Transfer Award for Outstanding Public Information. Mr. Kuhn holds a master's degree in Science Education from the University of Denver and a bachelor's degree in Aircraft Engineering Technology from Embry-Riddle Aeronautical University. He has taught science in grades 6–12, has been an assistant principal, and is listed in *Who's Who Among America's Teachers,* 7th and 9th editions. Before becoming an educator, Mr. Kuhn worked as an engineer and officer in the U.S. Army Reserve.

Kim Malenoski is a Lead Consultant for McREL's Educational Technology team. Her favorite part of the job is mentoring teachers one on one as they integrate technology in lessons. Ms. Malenoski holds a master's degree in Instructional Technology from National University at San Diego and a bachelor's degree in Education with a minor in Mathematics from the University of Northern Colorado. She taught elementary and middle school for seven years before she became a national trainer and project manager for an educational software company. She also spent time with the Colorado Department of Education, working with districts on technology planning, grants, and policy development.

Mid-continent Research for Education and Learning (McREL) is a Denver-based nonprofit education and research organization. For more than 40 years, McREL has been dedicated to helping educators use research to improve student achievement.

McREL offers in-depth professional development in connection with this book, both face to face and online. For more information, please visit www.mcrel.org/technology or send an e-mail to edtech@ mcrel.org.